CELEBRATING THE SUPER BOWL

PROGRAMS, PROFITS, PARTIES

CELEBRATING THE SUPER BOWL

PROGRAMS, PROFITS, PARTIES

LINDA K. FULLER

COMMON GROUND

First published in 2024
as part of the Insert Imprint Name Book Imprint
doi: 10.18848/978-1-963049-11-4/CGP (Full Book)

Common Ground Research Networks
60 Hazelwood Drive
Champaign, IL 61820 USA
Ph: +1-217-328-0405

Library of Congress Cataloging-in-Publication Data

Names: Fuller, Linda K., author.
Title: Celebrating the Super Bowl: Programs, Profits, Parties / Linda K.
   Fuller.
Description: Champaign, Illinois: Common Ground Research Networks, [2024]
   | Includes bibliographical references and index. | Summary: "A de facto American national holiday and phenomenon, the Super Bowl claims a spot as one of the most significant sporting events in the world and the most widely celebrated, feasted and feasting event of the year— with $14+ billion at stake, commercials costing $7 million for a 30-second spot, record-setting broadcast ratings, and 113+ million viewers. More avocados (105 million pounds) are consumed, and more beer is drunk (325 million gallons) on the single day of Superbowl Sunday. But there is much more at play than partying at our annual sports extravaganza, as this scholarly researched yet readable volume demonstrates: Here you will read a historical perspective that includes discussions of the meta-event's economics (stakeholders, host cities, advertising, gambling, and media), fandom, ratings, halftime entertainment, the roles of mythic spectacle and religion, football's sexist, militaristic language, gender issues like cheerleaders and sex trafficking, the Puppy Bowl, medical concerns like concussions and violence, tailgating and foodie ideas—all along with tidbits about your favorite team(s) and player(s). Touchdown!"-- Provided by publisher.
Identifiers: LCCN 2023053026 (print) | LCCN 2023053027 (ebook) | ISBN
   9781963049091 (hardback) | ISBN 9781963049107 (paperback) | ISBN
   9781963049114 (adobe pdf) | ISBN 9781963049121 (ebook)
Subjects: LCSH: Super Bowl. | United States--Social life and customs.
Classification: LCC GV956.2.S8 F85 2024 (print) | LCC GV956.2.S8 (ebook)
   | DDC 796.332/648--dc23/eng/20231213
LC record available at https://lccn.loc.gov/2023053026
LC ebook record available at https://lccn.loc.gov/2023053027

TABLE OF CONTENTS

PREFACE

Sitting here with my mug that says Super Bowl XL1/02 04 07 (Indianapolis Colts beating the Chicago Bears 29-17), a memento pushing Phoenix for the next year's contest, it strikes me how long I have been invested in this topic.

During the Persian Gulf War, when we even wondered whether Super Bowl XXV/1991 would be played, the militaristic language in its reportage struck me such that I co–content-analyzed that program and presented my findings—"Sportstalk/wartalk/patriotismtalk/mentalk: Super Bowl XXV" for the International Association for Mass Communication Research (IAMCR) at *Guarujá*, Brazil. Little has changed from the declaration that was made three decades ago: "Not the least of its attractions is the self-conscious hype that the Super Bowl draws, commanding equally lucrative pre- and post-game hoopla…The game itself is oftentimes hardly the point; rather, it is the parties, the people and, most importantly, the products surrounding it." Later, when invited by journalism professors Meta G. Carstarphen and Susan C. Zavoina to contribute to their book *Sexual Rhetoric: Sexuality, Gender, and Identity* (Greenwood Press 1999), came an opportunity to consider examples of intersections between women and the masculine language of sport and sportscasting, "Super Bowl speak" being the result. In the midst of examining how Super Sunday has become a highly hyped ratings leader, an unofficial national holiday, a feasting/partying/gambling event, as well as a bonanza for advertisers and media outlets, though, it struck me that the dark side(s) of Super Bowl also need to be analyzed and reported.

In 2015, at the Popular Culture Association (PCA) conference in New Orleans, LA, an editor expressed interest in publishing an early version of this study, but time and fortune got in the way; now, it could not be more exciting to at last be doing this book under the auspices of Patricia Alonso of Common Ground Research Networks (CGRN). What you are reading here has benefited greatly from both her interest and suggestions. Furthermore, let me thank Marty Triola, Professor Emeritus of Mathematics at Dutchess Community College and author of the *Triola Statistics Series* textbooks, for reading this section on gambling. Permit me to also include my family: While my husband, Eric, has been pivotal both for partying and proofing, each of our sons also has had various roles here. Our oldest, Will, was part of hologram covers for the NFL Super Bowl programs while working in the paper industry; the middle one, Keith, has been the brunt of kidding for his steadfast fandom for the Green Bay Packers; and the youngest, Alex, has been a stalwart supporter by doing copyediting of the manuscript and resolving computer issues.

It is tough for our family to remember when we did *not* either throw or go to a Super Bowl party. Early on, those parties usually involved other families and friends, oftentimes making for really large events. There were some years when we women staged our own, alternative fun and played tennis instead of staying home and watching television, but certain other years also stand out. Probably the craziest memory is from 1996, when I had a Fulbright teaching in Singapore and one of my colleagues at Nanyang Technological Institute invited a bunch of us "ex-pats" to his place on campus housing to watch the Dallas Cowboys beat San Francisco. We had all the trimmings from home: chips and dip, burgers, balloons, Coke, and camaraderie. Problem was, Singapore is famous for censorship, but we simply couldn't believe it when the entire televised game was over in twenty minutes as anything deemed "inappropriate"—cheerleaders, certain ads, risqué outfits, never mind sportscaster commentary—was deleted. The screen went blank, and we were left to thank our host and go home.

Another year stands out: Super Bowl XLVIII/2014, Seattle Seahawks vs. Denver Broncos, when we invited Rwandan friends to join us. Their initial reaction was overwhelmingly enthusiastic, especially as one of the teens knew that Bruno Mars was performing. But then there was a pause as, hesitatingly, another sister asked, "What *is* a Super Bowl?" We laughed, and still tease them about it, but the actual experience of our having to explain things was a helpful learning process all around.

When we moved to the Connecticut shore, right away we threw a party for our new neighbors to celebrate Super Bowl XL1X/2015, my favorite role being (re)match-making people of similar interests. For L1/2017, we knew many more people, and the invitation encouraged coming before kickoff and that "Au d'oeuvres will be accepted—if organic, local, LGBTIQ-friendly." One couple came with Patriot-painted faces, and another good friend still loves to rib us for having forty to fifty people with what she describes as "the smallest television of all time" (the actual screen is 28″ × 16′, but it gets smaller with each telling). That time, at least we had three or four other TVs all around the house (even smaller), and Lady Gaga at halftime was a great hit. Gladys Knight sang the national anthem, but Tom Brady was the star for our New England crowd. The Patriots tablecloth I made years ago has seen plenty of feasts, often holding my

Heart-Healthy Lasagna

4 lbs. ground turkey
2 to 3 onions, green peppers, and garlic, chopped
3 lb. tomatoes
32 oz. kidney beans, 16 oz. cannellini beans
10 oz. diced tomatoes and chilies
12 oz. tomato paste
2 cups chopped carrots and celery
1 tablespoon salt, 1 teaspoon pepper, 3 whole cloves, 2 tablespoons chili powder
Combine all ingredients in a large crockpot and cook 6 to 8 hours on low. (I often double this, in several pots, as you can always freeze leftovers.)

"Ladies only" was the theme for Super Bowl LV1/2022, when my husband parked cars and then went with his buddies while several dozens of us grazed, noshed, and enjoyed the wine bar while mostly only watching the game at half-time, when Mary J. Blige was joined by Dr. Dre, Snoop Dogg, Eminem, and Kendrick Lamar. Those who wanted to gamble were encouraged to bring $1 so the stakes were small but the fun and chit-chat were contagious.

Already you can see that this book ranges from the serious to the silly. Such is the topic of Super Bowl, considered here from historical, ecopolitical, sociocultural, as well as celebratory and linguistic perspectives. Consider it a metacritique of a meta-event.

As this book went to press, Super Bowl LV11 was played on February 12, 2023 at State Farm Stadium in Glendale, AZ, the Kansas City Chiefs triumphing over the Philadelphia Eagles 38-35 in what most viewers agreed was a great game. It had some statistics relevant to this study: The average ticket price was a whopping $6,400; it was the fourth competition to take place in the Phoenix metropolitan area; both teams came in with league-best records of 14-3 and both had Black quarterbacks (Jalen Hurts and Patrick Mahomes, the latter being named MVP), and female Navy flyers performed the flyover for the first time ever. Donna Kelce became the first mother to have two sons playing—if on two different teams, and Kylie Kelce's very pregnant wife brought her OB-GYN to the game just in case. Drawing 113M viewers in the United States alone by Kevin Burkhardt and Greg Olsen (my husband thrilled to get rid of Joe Buck)—along with being streamed to a huge international audience—it was the second most-watched television program after the July 20, 1969 Apollo 11 moon landing. The halftime show headlined by Rihanna drew 118.7M viewers, with the Barbadian singer/businesswoman later explaining her baby bump (National Review labeled it a "pro-life Super Bowl"). Broadcast by Fox in Dolby Vision high-dynamic range (HDR) with an exclusive on Xfinity, the network charged an all-time high of $7M/30-second ad, a Disney commemoration of its centennial garnering a five-star rating. American Sign Language (ASL) accompanied country's Chris Stapleton during the national anthem as well as for some other singers, and indigenous Arizona peoples were acknowledged during the festivities. Overall, as the *Republican-American* reported, Super Bowl LV11 was considered to have "feel-good vibes for all."

Linda K. Fuller
Madison, CT, 2024

## CHAPTER 1

Pre-Game Introduction to Celebrating the Super Bowl

Preparations

The Super Bowl, the championship game of American professional football, is the most watched, written about, and talked about single sports event in the United States today. It has become a national ritual, and Super Sunday is akin to a national holiday—marked by gatherings of family and friends, food, drink, and betting on the outcome.

—Ackley, Levinson, and Gems, "The Super Bowl: An American Institution."
(2019, 55)

Variously referred to as the biggest sporting event in the world, America's de facto national holiday, and/or "the most over-hyped event in human history" (Albom 2008, 6), the Super Bowl has become one of the most widely celebrated entertainment events of the year—and not just in the United States. Said to be watched by more people than those who vote in presidential elections (St. John 2010), it has become our second largest feasting day after Thanksgiving—when 46M pounds of avocados are consumed, something of a winter version of the Fourth of July. Popular wedding venues are available, and budget-conscious brides can count on smaller numbers—but who would even think about getting married that day? Word is that internet use is lower during Super Bowl than at any other time of the year except 4:00 a.m. on Christmas day. Celebratory drinking for at-risk men has been found to be particularly hazardous on Super Sunday (Dearing et al. 2014), and, according to Statista.com 2020, some 54 percent of Americans plan to attend a Super Bowl party. By default, we are encouraged to set aside resolutions such as dieting and, instead, fully participate today in anticipation of talking about it tomorrow. While some 47,000 party evites were reportedly sent out in 2009, now hundreds of choices for "connecting with friends" for The Big Game continue to evolve. As it turns out, our celebration of this iconic sports event is a bacchanalian combination of American commercial culture and inequities, along with balloons, buffalo chicken wings, betting, and beer.

A simple Google search of the term *Super Bowl* draws about 1,930,000,000 hits. Streamed in over 150 countries to some 20 to 30M global viewers (if sometimes edited or on tape-delay), it is destination, must-see TV: live, in real time, typically drawing more than half of all television households in the United States and attracting 187.3M multiplatform fans, women making up 47 percent of that number. If early games were decided by 10 points or more, the more recent trend has been toward much closer, heart-wrenching matches, with bookies enjoying the drama. Stanley D. Eitzen (2016, 8) has pointed out that "The Super Bowl brims with potential for great drama, heroics, disastrous errors, and excellence in performance, all of which are heightened by an uncertain outcome." The urban myth that sewers overflow at halftime is only half true, as water supply operators do report upticks during key times of the game, but prognostications of babies born in winning counties nine months after the Super Bowl have been discounted (Hayward and Rybinska 2017) and estimates of Monday morning hangovers remain elusive.

"America loves football," David Von Drehl (2014) declares, "from Turkey Day touch to Friday Night Lights, from State U. Saturdays to the NFL." And with love comes indulgence, a tolerance for ignoring the rules that govern the rest of us. "If one were to create from scratch a sport to reflect the sexual, racial, and organization priorities of the American power structure, it is doubtful that one could improve on football," Michael Real (1995, 107) concluded. Meanwhile, the National Football League (NFL) has been exempted from antitrust laws, shielded from tax collectors, and fattened by television moguls bearing billion-dollar contracts.

As indicated in "Appendix 5: Super Bowl Team Wins," the New England Patriots and the Pittsburgh Steelers are tied at six wins each, the Dallas Cowboys and the San Francisco 49ers following at five, New York Giants at four, Denver Broncos and Washington Redskins at three, Baltimore Ravens, Kansas City Chiefs, Miami Dolphins, and Oakland Raiders at two, ten others once, and nine none at all. But oftentimes it hardly matters who wins, since the main point is the celebration itself.

The Super Bowl is quite a ratings leader; Nielsen Media Research lists it as the top-rated television program—the years 1978, 1982, 1983, and 1986 accounting for the largest audiences of all time. And rates for advertisements continue to grow; consider commercials for the first Super Bowl—called the AFL-NFL World Championship; the Green Bay Packers vs. the Kansas City Chiefs cost $42,500 for the game played January 15, 1967 in Los Angeles, and the cost of a 30-second commercial in 2020 was $5.6M. Now, *Super Bowl Greatest Commercials* is a favorite television show unto itself, complete with its own website.

Miami, FL has hosted the Super Bowl the most, at eleven times—Super Bowl LV/2021 being the first and only time that a host city team has played in its own stadium, closely followed by New Orleans (ten times), then Pasadena, CA (five times), and other cities only a few times, each time gaining prestige and profits. According to Ticket IQ, ticket prices for the 2020 battle between the Kansas City Chiefs and the San Francisco 49ers were the most expensive ever, at an average of $10,835 (Buchwald 2020). Perhaps more amazingly, the demand for them exceeds the NFL's ability to provision all those who want to attend, only 1 percent being available to fans, through a random drawing.

Etsy suggests more than one hundred items priced under $30 for half-time parties, such as tanks and T-shirts declaring the wearer was "Just there for the commercials and snacks," care packages, Game Day menus, posters, underwear, football treats, and more. Pinterest displays thousands of Super Bowl foodie images: guacamole dips and salsas, entire nacho bars, appetizers and snacks like bacon-cheddar dip, tacos, or chocolate-covered pretzels, as well as heartier fare ranging from finger foods like Jalapeño popper turnovers or deep-fried pickles to BBQ beef sliders, pastrami sandwiches, Sloppy Joes, and Popcorn Chicken to Perfect Pina Coladas or laced lemonade. Buffalo chicken wings and pizza are a given; gluttony rules. (Small wonder that antacid sales spike by 20% the next day!) Desserts are another matter altogether, whether football-shaped cookies, cakes depicting entire stadiums, "deflategate" pops, chocolate fruit dips, Oreo football cookie balls, cookie-dough footballs, popcorn with team-appropriate colored M&Ms, and, of course, "football puppy chow" for canine accomplices. Posters prevail, whether crossword puzzles, picture-matching contests, Game Day apps, betting pools, banners, Bingo, goal post predictions, Super Bowl trivia, word scrambles, concession-stand evites, an NFL mascot matching game, or DIY football crafts. And then consider all those accessories, like drinking mugs with football insignias, nail polish, chocolate pops, penalty flags, candles, turf-like placements, touchdown banners, and Super Bowl–specific recipe books—never mind napkins, tablecloths, and any number of beer containers. Clearly, it has become deeply imbedded into our national popular culture.

"America's annual sports extravaganza" (Fuller 1999), the Super Bowl, has become the "Great American Time Out"; the most venerated day in the life of the American male; Prime Time for male bonding; the "most important single-day sporting event on the planet" (Weiss 2003); "our great national campfire, around which we cluster" (Will 2019) and America's biggest sports betting event—all on a single day, on a single stage. As early as 1974, Christian minister Norman Vincent Peale, author of *The Power of Positive Thinking*, declared that it had grown to such proportions that, "If Christ were alive today he'd be at the Super Bowl." And my favorite sportswriter, the late Frank Deford (2009), famously stipulated that, "Super Sunday isn't an official paid holiday, but let's face it: It has grown to become as much an accepted part of the modern American calendar as President's Day or Memorial Day."

Super Bowl (L1V, the fifty-fourth), played February 2, 2020 at Hard Rock Stadium in Miami Gardens, FL, had a local attendance of 62,417 and some notable parties before, during, and afterward; *Forbes* (Reimer 2020) declared it "the most political in history," the Trump presidency looming over militaristic pregame festivities, Latinx superstars Jennifer Lopez and Shakira at half-time, corporate social progressivism on full display, TurboTax spotlighting transgender actresses Trace Lysette and Isis King, and corporations co-opting social progress while Jay-Z sat during the national anthem. Taking its turn in a three-year rotation with CBS and NBC, the Fox network (along with Fox Deportes in Spanish) had a US television audience of 102M with a national Nielsen rating of 41.6 and it played digitally on Fox Sports' streaming platforms and the NFL and Yahoo! Sports apps. Its technical production was news in that the game could be seen in 4K ultra high-definition resolution and high dynamic range—considered "next-gen format" (Costa 2019) emphasizing instant stats as a means of encouraging fan engagement by means of 50 square meters of LED walls, twenty-five cameras, and the movable two-point Flycam. There were more than seven hours of pregame programming, at three different locales (South Beach, as well as inside and outside the stadium), including a Kickoff show, a four and half hour NFL Sunday show, and then the gonzo game itself starting at 6:30 p.m. Eastern Standard Time. Its official audience was said to be 102M, but *Sports Business Journal* reported the total audience was 135 to 140M, a Nielsen survey concluding that Super Bowl L1V had generated 35 percent to 40 percent more viewers per household than had the regular season and playoffs.

"There was a time when getting even the faintest whiff of a marketer's Super Bowl plans before game day was as feasible as getting water from a stone," Rae Ann Fera (2013) has said.

> The level of secrecy shrouding Super Bowl ads matched the grandiose specta-
> cle of America's biggest game. But all that's changed. Social media has ushered
> in a new reality for marketers looking to play in the big game, and it's allowing
> brands to create deeper narratives, engage fans earlier on and create greater
> buzz by releasing teasers and assets online before the event.

That is why this chapter is titled "Pre-game," introducing you to how the
Super Bowl has evolved into a major sporting and partying event. Increasingly, we continue to realize that it has become a unique phenomenon of
America's commercial, political, and popular culture (Kellner 2003; Wenner
1989)—a marketing bellwether of our times. Despite warnings that it can
even be a health risk, as all that emotional involvement that can lead to stress,
never mind "lack of sleep, overeating, wolfing down junk food, boozing and
smoking" (Ritter 2008). From various spectator and social scientific lenses,
it has been considered in terms of ritual—like Sally Jenkins' insights in *Men
Will Be Boys* (1996) or Michael L. Butterworth (2008) calling it a "distinctly
American ritual of excess," even religion (Price 2001; Real 1989) an indeli-
ble, incredibly important part of our popular culture.

Following a discussion describing the Super Bowl phenomenon, including a literature review and my interest in its underlying rhetoric, this book
will provide a brief history in Chapter 2, outline its ecopolitical issues (the
NFL, stakeholders, host cities, commercials, production, gambling, and the
role of media) in Chapter 3, sociocultural aspects (fandom, sexism, racism,
the role of ritual and religion, the violence factor, and football lingo) in
Chapter 4, parties (celebrity events, tailgates, potlucks, picnics, and general
pig-outs) in Chapter 5, and then draw some concluding thoughts on Super
Bowl in Chapter 6. The appendices include acronyms, Super Bowl–related websites, team-related references, and list of the championships, and
the extensive References should be helpful to both researchers and general
fans. The picture, it turns out, is not all frivolity and fun, but is also rife
with issues such as concussions, gambling, drugs, gender-based violence
(GBV), racial and sexist concerns. Overwhelmingly, through analyzing the
language of Super Bowl, we will see that it is much more than balloons, buffalo chicken wings, betting, and beer; in fact, it actually is all those aspects
and so much more.

The Super Bowl

> The Super Bowl is *the* game…No game has more TV viewers. No sports ticket costs more. No other halftime show is louder, brighter, wilder.
>
> —Dina Anastasio, *What Is the Super Bowl?* (2019, 1)

The Super Bowl, if it really needs a description/explanation, is an annual NFL championship contest that usually takes place in early February, the winner awarded the Vince Lombardi Trophy—named for the coach of the Green Bay Packers from 1959 to 1967, who won Super Bowls 1 and 2. Right off, it should be noted that the teams featured here are those that have played in the Super Bowl, listed here alphabetically:

Arizona Cardinals
Atlanta Falcons
Baltimore Colts
Baltimore Ravens
Buffalo Bills
Carolina Panthers
Chicago Bears
Cincinnati Bengals
Cleveland Browns
Dallas Cowboys
Denver Broncos
Green Bay Packers
Indianapolis Colts
Kansas City Chiefs
Los Angeles Raiders
Los Angeles Rams
Miami Dolphins
Minnesota Vikings
New England Patriots
New Orleans Saints
New York Giants
New York Jets
Oakland Raiders
Philadelphia Eagles

Pittsburgh Steelers
San Diego Chargers
San Francisco 49ers
Seattle Seahawks
St. Louis Rams
Tampa Bay Buccaneers
Washington Redskins (Note: The Washington Football Team as of 2020)

First played January 15, 1967 in Los Angeles, its official name was bestowed retroactively since it did not get the honorific *Super Bowl* until 1967. Representing the NFL in that initial game, the Green Bay Packers beat the American Football League (AFL)'s Kansas City Chiefs 35-10. As it turns out, that was the single time the game was simulcast by two networks, since NBC had the rights to AFL games (with Curt Gowdy and Paul Christman as announcers), CBS to the NFL's (and announcers Ray Scott, Jack Whitaker, and Frank Gifford). Nielsen ratings were high for both networks, CBS's being 22.6 (26.75M viewers) and NBC 18.5 (24.43M) for an estimated 51.18M viewers. Attendance was 61,946, the half-time show featuring Al Hirt and marching bands from the University of Arizona and Grambling State University, and Green Bay quarterback Bart Starr was voted MVP. It started a routine whereby the winning team gets a sterling silver trophy and every player on the winning team gets a diamond-studded ring. Chapter 2 is dedicated to a more detailed, if only brief, history of the Super Bowl.

A Review of the Literature on the Super Bowl

In 1975, Michael R. Real published his first iteration of "Super Bowl: Mythic spectacle" in the *Journal of Communication*, an analysis that begins with an introductory subtitle suggesting that "Analysis of a telecast finds in its expressions of values and functions of the larger social structure." Wondering even then about the determinants making the Super Bowl "the most lucrative annual spectacle in American mass culture," Real analyzed a videotape of Super Bowl VIII "as a para-literary text for exegesis." His thesis about the Super Bowl is three-fold: (1) (It) combines electronic media and spectator sports in a ritualized mass activity, (2) reveals specific cultural values proper to American institutions and ideology, and (3) is best explained as a contemporary form of mythic spectacle. Citing its success in a mere eight years, "the capstone of an empire," he cites some statistics, such as surpassing the 100-year-old Kentucky Derby and the 70-year-old World Series to become the Number One sports star–spangled spectacle in the United States as well as being the televised event of the year. Based on reportage from *Variety* and *Broadcasting*, these were the figures for 1974s telecast:

- Live attendance: 71,882
- Television audience: 70 to 95M
- CBS payment to NFL for television rights: $2,750,000
- CBS charge for advertising per minute: $200,000 to $240,000
- Total CBS advertising income from game: over $4,000,000
- Estimated expenditures in Houston by Super Bowl crowd: $12,000,000
- Newsmen covering: over 1,600
- Words of copy sent out from newsmen: over 3,000,000

Interviewed some four decades later (Dheensaw 2015), when he was a professor of communications and culture at Royal Roads University, Victoria, BC, Real saw the Super Bowl as still "Huge…from all the different levels and to the passion people bring to it, you can see how it adds up…When people asked me then if it could get any bigger, I couldn't have imagined how." Who could ever have imagined audiences of more than 100M, television rights of $3B, NFL profits of more than $5B, or $5.6M for a thirty-second commercial?

When Super Bowl XXVI came to her hometown of Minneapolis in 1992, Dona Schwartz (1997, 2) decided to study the "crafted spectacle, an American rite" that accompanied all the hoopla of being a host city. Organizing a team of photojournalists to check out its effects on the citizenry, she found that the Super Bowl is used by CEOs "as a vehicle to cement deals, entertain clients, reward productive employees with a free excursion, and simultaneously create tax deductions"—at the expense of taxpayers, women and minorities especially, affected by what she termed the media orgy.

As you might imagine, there are numerous books specifically about the NFL (e.g., Billick and MacCambridge 2009; Crepeau 2014; Eisenberg 2018; Feinstein 2008; Glauber 2018; Griffith 2012; Harris 1986; Horrigan 2019; Jaworski, Plaut, and Cosell 2010; Jozsa Jr. 2010; Leibovich 2018; Oriard 1998, 2010; Rice and Williams 2019). Football per se is covered by both practitioners and academics (e.g., Cook 2012; Dawidoff 2013; Felser 2008; Gargano 2010; Gems and Pfister 2019; Leiger 2011; MacCambridge 2005), and there are a few books out there about Super Bowl anniversaries (e.g., Fischer 2015; Fleder 2019; Maki and Naylor 2016; McGinn 2012).

There have been some notable books about specific Super Bowl teams, such as for Baltimore, with Jack Gilden (2018) writing about the role of the Colts' Johnny Unitas and Don Shula relative to the formation of the NFL, Michael Olesker (2008) about how the team was supported by the city, and then Dean Smith (2013) on fandom for the Baltimore Ravens. The Kent State University has produced several important works, such as Watkins and Maloney (2018) on the Cincinnati Bengals, and Gordon (2017), Harris (2018), and Knight (2003, 2006, 2015) about the Cleveland Browns. Matt Erlich's 2019 study of Kansas City vs. Oakland rivalry as well as Gruver and Campbell's (2019) discussion on the rivalry between the Oakland Raiders and Pittsburgh Steelers are exemplary works, as is C. Richard King's 2016 study of racial insults and cultural appropriation relative to the team known, until 2020, as the Washington Redskins.

Many are directed at younger audiences, such as Dina Anastasio's 2019 *What Is the Super Bowl?* or Matt Christopher's *The Super Bowl: Legendary Sports Events* (2006) and others by various publishers like Firefly Books, Penguin Workshop, Creative Education, or Little, Brown Books for Young Readers. And then there is almost an industry around books aimed at "helping" women understand the game, such as Suzy Beamer Bohnert's *Game-Day Goddess: Learning Football's Lingo* (2007); Suzanna Gagnier's *Putting on the Blitz: The Football Book for Women* (2007); Mariah Burton Nelson's 1994 classic *The Stronger Women Get, the More Men Love Football: Sexism and the American Culture of Sports*; A. J. Newell's ("The Football Dude") *Gaga for Gridiron: The Ultimate Guide to Football for Women* (2012); Holly Robinson Peete's and Daniel Paisner *Get Your Own Damn Beer, I'm Watching the Game!: A Woman's Guide to Loving Pro Football* (2005); or Teresa Saucedo-Artino's *Football for Females: The Women's Survival Guide to the Football Season* (2000).

There are literally hundreds of books about the Super Bowl, and Chapter 6 lists only a sampling of nearly six hundred team-related citations. Additionally, there are several hundred more books that are simply statistical or trivia questions or are directed at young readers or might even be made up of dirty jokes about certain NFL teams.

Most books about the Super Bowl predictably are event-specific, for example, James Aron (2011) *Breakthrough 'Boys: The Story of the 1971 Super Bowl Champion Dallas Cowboys* or Mike Freeman (2012) *Undefeated: Inside the 1972 Miami Dolphins' Perfect Season*. There are some that are athlete- or coach-specific—Bendetson and Marshall (2010) *When the Cheer-ing Stops: Bill Parcells, the 1990 New York Giants, and the Price of Great-ness*; Sean Glennon (2012) *Tom Brady vs. the NFL: The Case for Football's Greatest Quarterback*; Adam Lazarus (2012) *Best of Rivals: Joe Montana, Steve Young, and the Inside Story Behind the NFL's Greatest Quarterback Controversy*; Vince Lombardi Jr. (2004) *The Lombardi Rules*; team-specif-ic—Chuck Carlson (2009) *Green Bay Packers: Yesterday & Today*; Roger Craig and Matt Maiocco (2012) *Tales from the San Francisco 49ers Side-line*; Matt Fulks (2008) *The Good, the Bad & the Ugly: Heart-Pounding, Jaw-Dropping, and Gut-Wrenching Moments from Pittsburgh Steelers Histo-ry*; Joe Nick Patoski (2012) *The Dallas Cowboys: The Outrageous History of the Biggest, Loudest, Most Hated, Best Loved Football Team in America*; Jim Wexell (2011) *Pittsburgh Steelers: Men of Steel*; or place-specific—Jim Dent (2011) *Super Bowl Texas Style*; John Eisenberg (2012) *Ten-Gallon War: The NFL's Cowboys, the AFL's Texans, and the Feud for Dallas's Pro Football Future*; Jeff Pearlman (2009) *Boys Will Be Boys: The Glory Days and Party Nights of the Dallas Cowboys Dynasty*.

In 1991, Pete Rozell—who described the Super Bowl as "the last chapter of a hair-raising mystery. No one would miss it," wrote *Super Bowl: Celebrating a Quarter Century of America's Greatest Game*, a reminiscence of his nearly three-decade-long stint as the commissioner of the NFL. Since then, there have been several histories as noted previously, most of them heavily illus-trated volumes. Allen St. John's *The Billion-Dollar Game: Behind the Scenes of the Greatest Day in American Sport—Super Bowl Sunday* (2010), while dated, is perhaps the best expose out there, underscoring the economics of "the biggest cultural phenomenon in American sports." Still, as sportswriter Joe Queenan (2009) points out, emphasizing owners, broadcasters, and pro-moters of the game is far less exciting than behind-the-scenes stories of play-ers and plays: "It's like paying homage to the guys who built the colosseum, but giving short shrift to the gladiators who brought in the crowds." While all of these books are included in appendices and/or References, none comes close to my study here, underscoring how popular a topic this is and why it is worth celebrating.

Theories and the Language of Super Bowl

Words are very low on the list of things men like to say. They speak in codes, terms, euphemisms, diagrams, epigrams, and clichés, but rarely do they make clear, simple statements in comprehensible language. The terminology of football demonstrates that, left to themselves, without women around to force them to elaborate, men would all end up talking to each other via signal lamps and X's and O's.

—Sally Jenkins, *Men Will Be Boys* (1996, 82).

Fascinated with the gendered language laced throughout sport—especially football—my developing theory of Gendered Critical Discourse Analysis (GCDA) is an ideal way to examine the Super Bowl. While at the same time recognizing norms and power plays between the sexes, it encourages sensitization to the rhetoric we use relative to the pervasiveness and salience of sport and the many social issues surrounding it. Check out the language in this volume to see how it underscores the argument of how connected sports talk is with militaristic and/ or sexist terms. Spiced with metaphors from our daily lives, sport rhetoric ranges from talk about playing hardball to sticky wickets to cheap shots. Routinely, we talk about offensive and defensive tactics, game plans, Monday morning quarterbacking, being team players, playing tough, playing fair, and more. Mediasport, dominated by an Old Boy's network with its own vocabulary, begs interpretation.

If we can't talk the talk, we are denied access to "level playing fields." Whether in our military-industrial complexes or our personal, sexual lives, the rhetoric of sport plays a critical role. My interest in this topic dates to 1992, and that research hooked me to learn more about the mix of militaristic and sexist terms in the commentary of football's ultimate competition, such as the following:

Wartalk

Two rigid, rampart-like lines of human flesh have been created, one of defense, the other of offense, and behind the latter is established a catapult to fire through a porthole opened in the offensive rampart a missile composed of four or five human bodies globulated about a carried football with a maximum of initial velocity against the presumably weakest point in the opposing rampart.

—Benjamin Ide Wheeler 1906, cited in James Weeks, "Football as a Metaphor for War." *American Heritage* 39 (6), 1988

"The language of violence is most clearly crystallized in the language of football, a language that reflects the masculinist history of sport," Jeffrey o. Segrave (1997, 5) states, "a language, as a result, alive with military metaphor." Here are some examples of militaristic "sportspeak": *blitz* (from the German *blitzkrieg*, a term referring to the advance of Hitler's troops into 1939 Poland), *bombs and bomb squads, offense/defense, flanks, victories and defeats, casualties, chucking, cleating, killing, hitting, holding, hooking, ammunition, weapons, taking aim, fighting, detonating, squeezing the trigger*, and *dominating*. Other terms included phrases like "blockading the way," "ground and air attacks," "fighting and dying on the frontlines," and "battling in the trenches." Strategies and tactics included *offenses, sticking to a game plan*, using "two-minute drills," *kamikaze squads*, or the "two-platoon system," "weaving through minefields," sometimes being reduced to employing "unnecessary roughness," even having sportscasters and newscasters use "telestrators" for charting movements. Mandelbaum (2020) says that, in this age of drones, "Football is war between individual men." He expands on how football vocabulary draws from the terminology of war:

> From a distance, a football game resembles a pre-modern battle: two groups of men in uniforms, wearing protective gear, crash into each other. Like most military battles, football is a contest for territory, with each team trying to advance the ball to the opposing side's goal. In football, as in war, older men draw up plans for younger, more vigorous men to carry out: The sport's coaches are its generals, the players its troops. Football teams mirror the tripartite organization of classical armies: the beefy linemen correspond to the infantry; the smaller, lighter players who actually carry the ball are the equivalent of cavalry; and the quarterback who advances the ball by throwing it through the air and the receivers who catch it are the sport's version of an army's artillery.

The essence of football is a competition to reach a goal(post), coached and flanked along by drill teams that serve as infantry for the troops. As in all armies, there is a ranking order and general orders for what is to be done from scrimmages to touchdowns.

Sextalk

Think of what a sexualized vocabulary is used in football—terms like "going all the way"; *pinching, squeezing, pumping*; "deep penetration"; "grinding it out"; "clutch plays"; using "bump and run" stratagem; "gang-tackling"; "naked reverses"; and "belly-backing" techniques. Sometimes there are *fumbles, huddles, hurry-up offenses, quick hits or releases*, or even "fakes." *Kicking* is key. No sport, I have argued, "better exemplifies the nexus of Big Business, big stakes, and big boys than American football." In general, for "going all the way," this language is particularly relevant to football. Strategically, the goal of American football seems pretty basic: eleven players on each team, *offense* or *defense*, try to reach *end zones* where they can *score*. The team with the most points wins. The ball, sometimes (erroneously) referred to as the pigskin, is handled by a ballcarrier, who hopes to keep it away from ball hawks. There might be body blocking, butt blocking, chop blocking, power blocking, roughing a kicker or passer, ball stripping, zone blocking, flea flicking, spiking, and encroaching or eating the ball. A player might be a headhunter, a heavy hitter, a scrimmager, a sledgehammer, a jumper, a monster, a punishing runner, or a punter. Opponents are always on the lookout for weak sides. He—and it always is a "he"—might deliberately spear a fellow player's helmet, make a sucker play, sack or shank the ball, make a plunge, or tackle a ballcarrier. There are even some ghoulish terms, a coffin corner being one of four places where sidelines and goal lines intersect, a dead-ball (one out of play) and dead-man (or sleeper) play referring to an illegal pretense for passing. A dying quail, when a toss lacks speed and power, can also be called a duck ball. Skull sessions, also known as chalk talk, review and predict plays. At the other extreme, how does one explain that football lingo also includes "Hail Mary," a low-percentage desperation pass that appeals to a higher power for completion? It may not surprise you that there can be intentional grounding, intercepts, slashing, "unsportsmanlike conduct," and a disabled list. Possession is of prime importance.

The classic notion of sexual progression takes on new meaning in football jargon, the 10-yard line meaning "holding hands," 20-yard "hugging," 30 "a kiss on the cheek," *40* the lips, *midfield* "tongue kissing." It progresses from there, the *40-yard line* when the shirt and bra are off, the *30-yard line* all off, the 20-yard line getting or giving oral sex. At the *first-and-goal* you really should have a condom, the *goal line* being a touchdown. (Do I need to spell that out?) The *kickoff* makes the first move (asking for a date), and a *kick return* asking how far you got on that date. *Downs* deal with how far your "attempts" went, *tumbles* with impotence, and *interceptions* question homosexuality. *Turnovers* mean anal sex, *field goals* when one partner has an orgasm, *touchdown* both, and a "high-scoring game" connotes multiple orgasms. A *pile-up* designates an orgy, "center" doggie-style, "tight end" is self-explanatory, a *wide end* being the opposite, *roughing* making us think of S&M, and you can only imagine what a "missed field goal" might mean. Offsides signify premature ejaculations, and, if you believe it, the various football bowls even have sexual connotations, the Rose Bowl's being romance, Citrus safe sex, Peachy juicy/wet sex, Fiesta sex in South America, and the Hula Bowl simply asks you to use your imagination.

"The Super Bowl discursive formation is remarkably complex," O'Donnell and Spires (2008) have noted,

> consisting not only of the match commentary and the ads, but also all the other elements which go to make its televised version—lasting on average some seven hours—unique: the pre-match show, the singing of the national anthem, the half-time show, the sideline interviews, the on-screen graphics, not to mention the intense media coverage before and after the game, the innumerable conversations among fans and so on.

My gendered sporting rhetorical analyses, always performed with inter-coder reliability, continue to help explain the wider sociocultural implications of sport. It finds that, although the Super Bowl appeals to a wide public, it fulfills private needs for entertainment.

In 2005, nine DC Divas from the National Women's Football Association (NWFA) decided to form an all-star team to take on men's football in a battle of the sexes—called *The Gender Bowl* (McDowell and Schaffner 2011), produced by Joel Raatz, the reality show pictured (arrogant) men vs. women discourses of conservative gender relations evidenced in these ways: (1) expressions of perceived biological differences, (2) references to women lacking football cultural capital, (3) the reiteration of gender stereotypes, and (4) the use of asymmetric denotations to reference men and women. As it turned out, women scored a touchdown in the final minute, but then the men scored another one, and no replay could declare a winner. Their conclusions: "The discourse of egalitarianism in *The Gender Bowl* is manifested through discourses that support perceived biological gender similarities and the struggle for equal opportunities." Rematch, anyone?

A Uniquely American Phenomenon

> The Super Bowl is not just *a* big event, it is the *biggest*. It is not just the final game, it is the ultimate spectacle. In the US, the Super Bowl is what Christmas is to shopping, Thanksgiving is to eating, New Year's Eve is to champagne and

hangovers, and the Fourth of July is to patriotism and fireworks. In combining all these attributes, the Super Bowl has become America's most complete celebration of itself.

—Real and Wenner, *Super Bowl: Mythic Spectacle Revisited* (2017, 200).

We Americans love sport; in fact, it is kind of a national obsession, as we use it for our tribal "social glue," for our cathartic experiences, our loyalties, and our hopes and dreams. We tend to value sports heroes over intellectuals, to be totally absorbed by sports media, and to know more about sports celebrities than our own neighbors, or oftentimes even our own families. But most of all, we Americans love football. Baseball may be touted as our national pastime, and the NBA draws crowds of more than 14,000 fans, but football continues to come in First Place for popularity. For many Americans, that love affair begins with hometown interest—maybe with high school football pep rallies and the glitz and glamour of homecoming games. It continues to grow, exponentially, reaching its peak each year with the ecstasy of Super Sunday as the deciding championship is played out at a fever-pitch frenzy before global audiences and tens of thousands of partygoers. "Although mass-mediated culture tends to profane a civilization's most sacred and powerful words and images," Michael R. Real (1975, 96) has noted, "in the process it manages to elevate otherwise mundane events of no real consequence to the status of spectacles of a powerful, quasi-sacred myth and ritual nature. The Super Bowl telecast conveys this feeling of larger-than-life drama." Clearly, it has become our national ritual.

With commercials costing $5.5M for a thirty-second spot, record-setting broadcast ratings, and 110+M consumers watching—and partying—our annual sports extravaganza known as the Super Bowl is uniquely American. In her 2006 insightful book *Dancing in the Streets: A History of Collective Joy*, Barbara Ehrenreich has outlined how games serve as a source of communal élan, sporting events as "a medium for generating collective thrills" (226) and how nationalism prevails along with pageantry. Pre-game there may be military flyovers, pep rallies honoring America, the Pledge of Allegiance, and other patriotic displays that continue throughout the day. "Games, we realize, are being enacted for consumers of sport," Fuller (2009) has noted, adding that,

> Analogies again can be made to theatre, as people pay a price to participate in visual displays. Suspended judgments encourage spectators to see the athlete in action, perhaps discounting what s/he may know about off-the-field stories. Sporting games have heroes and heroines, villains and the victorious, underdogs

and umbrage, triumph and trial, drama and denouement. But basically, we all
play to win. And to have fun. But basically, we all play to win. And to have fun.

And fun we have with the Super Bowl.

Here, the notion of celebration begins by introducing the Super Bowl as a
mega-event, then supplying a brief history of the game. As economics is at its
core, next come discussions on stake holders, host cities, advertising, the many
festivities involved, gambling, and the role of media in terms of ratings, sportscasting and sportscasters, and social media. Sociocultural aspects—fandom,
sexism, racism, ritual and religion, violence, and the language of football—provide a darker side to our understanding this cultural institution that has become
an unofficial national holiday whereby 1.5M Americans call in "sick" the next
day (costing employers more than $3B) and another 4.4M show up late for
work. Hopsicker and Dyreson (2017) phrase it this way:

> A half-century after the NFL's first attempt at adorning its season-culminating
> championship football game with a spectacular atmosphere, Super Bowl LI
> demonstrated that the venture has become more than just a game. The Super
> Bowl is now an American institution, producing an experience that exudes the
> qualities of a quintessential American holiday—a holiday that, paradoxically, fre-
> quently seems to treat the NFL's championship game as an ancillary to the festiv-
> ities. In the five decades between Super Bowl I and Super Bowl LI, the popularity
> of Super Bowl Sunday has exploded. It has become the largest shared experience
> within the national culture. More Americans watch the Super Bowl than vote in
> elections, attend religious services, or commemorate patriotic sacrifices.

When the date falls, the partying itself is yet another key aspect, whether sponsored by celebrities and/or corporations or taking place as tailgates, potlucks, picnics or general pig-outs, Super Bowl Sunday has become a special day unto itself.
Also, it behooves me to delineate what this book is *not* about: While the analysis
is academically based, it wants to go beyond stories and statistics to determine
what it is about us as a people and us as a country that our idea of celebrating
involves a bunch of head-butting, testosterone-driven men chasing a ball.

All these topics, and no doubt many more, promise quite a story in the telling
of how the Super Bowl is celebrated. That celebration, it should be emphasized,
is a critical lens through which to realize what an American cultural event the
game is—historically, economically, and socioculturally. Hoping that you will
not be disappointed if your favorite players, coaches, teams, and/or topics are
not discussed, let me encourage you to let me know your reaction(s).

## CHAPTER 2

A Brief History of the Super Bowl

The first Super Bowl, from 1967, was introduced in Chapter 1, the Green Bay Packers representing the NFL and beating the AFL's Kansas City Chiefs 35-10. Officially called the AFL-NFL World Championship, it pitted legendary coaches Vince Lombardi (Green Bay) and Hank Stram (Kansas City) against one another. "Top tickets at Los Angeles Coliseum were selling for twelve dollars," Dina Anastasio (2019, 7) reminds us, adding that, "In 1967, that price seemed crazy to most people. Who could afford that much for a ticket to a football game? There were empty seats. The game would turn out to be the only Super Bowl in history that wasn't sold out." Michael MacCambridge (2005), author of *America's Game*, supplies the story behind the name Super Bowl:

> When the established National Football League merged with the upstart American Football League in June 1966, football fans finally got their wish—a showdown…Later that summer, AFL founder Lamar Hunt sent a memo to NFL Commissioner Pete Rozelle suggesting that the merged leagues should coin a phrase for the new game. "I have kiddingly called it the Super Bowl," Hunt wrote, "which obviously can be improved upon." Rozelle, with his background in journalism and PR, never cared for the name, deeming it unsophisticated. But even before the first game was, Hunt's title swept through the football, news media and advertising worlds. By the end of 1966, network executives were referring to the day of the first game as "Super Sunday."

At that first game of January 15, 1967 in Los Angeles, before a crowd of 61,946, historian Michael Beschloss (2015) tells us, that there was a struggle over the choice of ball:

> The A.F.L.'s football (manufactured by Spalding) was a quarter-inch longer, slightly narrower and more tacky on its surface than the N.F.L.'s ball (made by

Wilson). The A.F.L.'s ball was said to be easier to pass, the N.F.L.'s more kick-able. As a compromise, each team was authorized to use its own football while on offense. This didn't become much of a controversy because, by modern stan-dards, Super Bowl I (as it is now called) was modest and quaint.

Tickets ranged from $6 to $12, and more than 35,000 seats were empty. The television viewership was estimated to be 60.

A basically combative competition, American football has its roots in rugby, by way of soccer, an extremely rough sport that dates from 1314 Britain; by way of example, Eric Dunning (2003, 46) cites a 1602 report by Sir Richard Carew about players "retyring home as from a pitched battaile, with bloody pates, bones broken and out of joynt, and such bruises as serve to shorten their daies." Acknowledging Allison Danzig's *The History of American Football* (1956) and David Nelson's *Anatomy of a Game: Football, the Rules and the Men Who Made the Game* (1994), Frank Francisco (2016, 1) has a fascinating take in *Evolution of the Game: Chronicle of American Football*:

> Long before there was the no-huddle, offense, before there was the Nickel de-fense, and before there was the zone blitz, there was the Chinese game of Tsu Chu (cuju). Military manuals dating to 2000 BC indicate that Chinese soldiers used Tsu Chu, played with a stuffed leather ball using the feet, as a physical activity.

Yale halfback Walter Camp is credited with transforming the game in the 1880s such that it became an intercollegiate and then a professional sport. By 1905, eighteen fatalities and 159 serious injuries had been reported, *The World* of New York claiming football as "the most brutal, perilous, and unnecessary sport sanctioned by any country in the world" (cited in Considine 1982, 123). Dave Revsine (2014, 3) writes that the formative period of American football took place between 1890 and 1915, "a big business…driven largely by the social elite," while Gerald R. Gems (2000) encourages us to consider how the history of football also includes that of militarism, leadership training, multicultural-ism, even feminism. The XFL (for "eXtreme Football League") was introduced in 2001, six days after Super Bowl XXXV, as the brainchild of Vince McMahon of the World Wrestling Federation (WWF). The Library of Congress and Susan Reyburn's *Football Nation* (2013) traces the game to colonial days, claiming that aspects such as fight songs, cheerleading, tailgating, cartoons, and other memorabilia all preceded its embrace as a college sport. "Collegians created the game and were the focus of popular attention until well after World War 11,"

James E. Herget (2013, v) prefaces his history of American football, adding that "Of course, we now have flag football, high school football, pee-wee football, Warner league football, six-man football, women's football, and arena (indoor) football."

Associated from the start with "manly men," American football history began at the college level, Yale vs. Princeton's 1873 match setting the stage for what stands today for the Pittsburgh Steelers vs. Baltimore Ravens, Green Bay Packers vs. Chicago Bears, New York Giants vs. Philadelphia Eagles, and Oakland Raiders vs. Kansas City Chiefs, to name a few. Rules for the game have evolved over time, Richard Crepeau (2014, 4) making the point that, early on, "Following the college football crisis of 1905 precipitated by eleven deaths on the field of play, the schools adopted rule changes designed to make the game safer and more attractive to spectators." Gems and Pfister (2009, 141) point out that football in the United States began in the post–Civil War era, in the midst of societal changes from agrarianism to industrialism, moving into modernization and urbanization at the same time as "struggles between the classes and the races, including the confrontations with and the integration of numerous and various groups of immigrants." American identity was developing and men ruled, and football a natural reflection of manliness and militaristic propensities.

Player/sportscaster Frank Gifford and Peter Richmond (2008) claims that the 1958 NFL championship, the New York Giants vs. the Baltimore Colts, the first sudden-death contest, "riveted the nation and helped propel football to the forefront of the American sports landscape." Taking place before 64,000 fans, millions more on their televisions, that contest is considered by some to be "the best ever" (see Bowden 2009). Of course, in the early days, television was so expensive that only the wealthy and sports bars could afford them, so it was a natural that people would congregate to watch the game, pro football and television ownership both taking off in the 1960s. Now, there are whole programs geared to how sports bars can best market themselves for Super Sunday. Cook (2012) calls those early days "rowdy, reckless," comparing pro football's time to that of adolescence—raging, hormonal, hairy, druggy, with coaches like John Madden and Bill Walsh (Walsh, Jamison and Walsh 2009) trying to outsmart one another.

Once the AFL and the NFL agreed to merge for the 1970 season, it was decided to follow Lamar Hunt's idea of using gladiatorial-reminiscent Roman numerals as designations for each game, Super Bowl V/1971 setting the standard with the earlier games retitled. Super Bowl 50/2016 was the exception—NFL designers apparently thinking that "L" by itself was unattractive, unmarketable for what was a year-long celebration described by Gallagher and Martin (2017) that had $30M in pledges before it began. Of the 71,088 fans on hand for the event, the word according to ESPN.com is that they bought 8,000 glasses of wine, ate 3,000 "Big 5-0 Sausages," 26,000 regular and 1,000 vegan hot dogs, and overall spent $152.28/person, or $10.83M in all (Breech 2016).

The national anthem has been part of the entertainment from the start, marching bands from Arizona and Michigan joining the UCLA choir in 1967, then moving to celebrities like Doc Severinsen in 1970 and Charley Pride in 1974. In 1977, Vikki Carr made news by singing *America the Beautiful*, but most stars have stuck to *The Star-Spangled Banner*—a Who's Who of key performers: Cheryl Ladd 1980, Helen O'Connell 1981, Diana Ross 1982, Leslie Easterbrook 1983, Barry Manilow 1984, San Francisco Boys Chorus 1985, Wynton Marsalis 1986, Neil Diamond 1987, Herb Alpert 1988, Billy Joel 1989, Aaron Neville 1990, Whitney Houston 1991, Harr Connick Jr. 1992, Garth Brooks 1993, Natalie Cole 1994, Kathie Lee Gifford 1995, Vanessa Williams 1996, Luther Vandross 1997, Jewel 1998, Cher 1999, Faith Hill 2000, Backstreet Boys 2001, Mariah Carey 2002, The Chicks 2003, Beyonce 2004, military choirs 2005, Aaron Neville and Aretha Franklin 2006, Billy Joel 2007, Jordin Sparks 2008, Jennifer Hudson 2009, Carrie Underwood 2010, Christina Aguilera 2011, Kelly Clarkson 2012, Alicia Keys 2013, Renee Fleming 2014, Idina Menzel 2015, Lady Gaga 2016, Luke Bryan 2017, Pink 2018, Gladys Knight 2019, Demi Lovato 2020, Jazmine Sullivan and Eric Church 2021. There was a bit of a scandal recently when deaf artist Christine Sun Kim, who signed for the hearing impaired at Super Bowl L1V/2020, claimed that Fox Sports cut her performance to only a few seconds.

"The National Football League that celebrated its first Super Bowl in 1967 bore scant resemblance to the league of its obscure origins," read the description of Craig R. Coenen's *From Sandlots to the Super Bowl: The National Football League, 1920–1967* (2005); it expands on that introduction:

> In its earliest years, the league was a ragtag collection of locally supported small-town teams that generated attention only in the locales in which they played, if they were lucky. Many teams received no support at all. Only after enduring a slow, often treacherous, journey did the enterprise of professional football reach its position as the king of the sports world by the late 1960s... Coenen recounts the NFL's ascension from a cash-strapped laughingstock to a perennial autumn obsession for millions of sports fans. It offers an in-depth summary of the NFL's early years and its struggles to build an identity...(and) documents how the NFL mastered the use of new technologies like television to market itself, generate new revenue, and to secure its financial future.

By the time of Super Bowl IV/1970, Richard Crepeau (2017, 10) has noted, the party atmosphere was growing, and New Orleans provided the ideal venue: "There were 3,000 pigeons and one turtle dove released during pre-game ceremonies; a tableaux of the Battle of New Orleans and a Mardi Gras parade…It was called the second largest bash in America, second only to Mardi Gras." The bar was set for celebrating. Super Bowl was ready to go from just being a sports event to becoming a mega partying event, to living up to its designation as "Super."

Starting in 2004, the game was set to be played the first Sunday in February to accommodate the NFL schedule. Hopsicker and Dyreson (2017) updated those early days to report that, more than a half century later, the pre-game show ran for hours before kickoff, attendees numbered 70,000 while viewers were estimated at 111M, college marching bands were replaced by Lady Gaga, and thirty-second ads ran at $5M. By the time of Super Bowl L1/2017, they declared the Super Bowl had become "an American institution, producing an experience that exudes the qualities of a quintessential American holiday—a holiday that, paradoxically, frequently seems to treat the NFL's championship game as an ancillary to the festivities." Lots of credit goes to Don Weiss (1926–2003), P/R director of the NFL who is known as the "sculptor of the Super Bowl"; Weiss (2003, vii), the ultimate insider, declared that "The Super Bowl draws the masses…it clearly has established itself as the most important single-day sporting event in the United States, if not in the world."

The NFL

> The National Football League has become a capitalist behemoth where millionaire players argue with billionaire owners over how best to divide the overflow of riches.
>
> —Gems and Pfister, *Touchdown: An American Obsession Goes Global* (2019, ix)

Backing up a bit, it may be helpful to review the fact that the NFL—the world's wealthiest and highest attended sports league, is made up of thirty-two teams divided into the two conferences of the American Football Conference (AFC) and the National Football Conference (NFC) that, in turn, are divided into four divisions:

AFC: AFC North, AFC South, AFC East, AFC West
NFC: NFC North, NFC South, NFC East, NFC West

Stay with me here, because while there are four teams in each division, those four teams play each other twice per season in addition to playing teams outside their divisions and conferences. Then too there are pre-season games before the sixteen regularly scheduled games, each team getting a "bye" of a week off per season and two "wild card" teams in the playoffs that determine which teams will play in the Super Bowl. If it seems that there are a lot of football games leading up to the annual championship known as Super Bowl, you are correct.

Don't ignore the fact that the NFL is an enormously lucrative business, having grown to mythic proportions. It draws revenue from a number of sources: NFL Enterprises (including the pay-television NFL Network, part of NFL Media: NFL.com, NFL Films [see Vogan 2014], NFL Now, NFL Mobile, and NFL RedZone, as well as NFL Sunday Ticket), NFL Ventures (for merchandising), plus television contracts. Television rights for the Super Bowl rotate on a three-year basis between CBS, Fox, and NBC under a contract worth $27B that will run through the 2022 season, ESPN's cost being $1.9B. Money underscores much of the enterprise, as rookies learn early on when they find themselves in a kind of hazing whereby they might be expected to pick up the tab for a group of players in excess of $20,000—exorbitant habits and rituals that become part of the package.

"The NFL is one of the most significant engines of contemporary culture, attracting legions of devoted fans, tens of millions of television viewers, and billions of dollars in annual revenue," Oates and Furness (2014, 3) have noted. "Indeed, the NFL has played and continues to play a formidable role in shaping not only the economics and aesthetics of professional sports in the United States but also the very contours of modern sport itself." Dominating any competition as America's most popular, successful sports league, the NFL's story, according to Joe Horrigan (2019, ix), former executive director of the Pro Football Hall of Fame, is extraordinary: "From its humble beginnings in small-town American in the 1920s to its present-day status as a multibillion-dollar industry, the NFL is an important and influential part of the multihued fabric of our society. Its rags-to-riches story and unrivaled popularity border on the unbelievable."

While our national sport continues to come under scrutiny from many sources—including scandals and institutionalized secrets, cheating, gambling, insane salaries for administrators and players, taxpayer-subsidized stadiums, controversies like "deflategate," and accusations of fostering a tolerance for violence and greed, our unofficial national holiday known as the Super Bowl nevertheless can be interpreted as a role model of self-disciplined athletes and their teamwork. As an aside, if you are interested in American football before the Super Bowl, let me recommend the following, listed chronologically: Robert W. Peterson's *Pigskin: The Early Years of Pro Football* (1997); Don Weiss and Chuck Day's *The Making of the Super Bowl: The Inside Story of the World's Greatest Sporting Event* (2002); Craig R. Coenen's *From Sandlots to the Super Bowl: The National Football League, 1920–1967* (2005); Larry Felser's *The Birth of the New NFL: How the 1966 NFL/ AFL Merger Transformed Pro Football* (2008); Chris Willis' *The Man Who Built the National Football League: Joe F. Carr* (2010); Michael Oriard's *Brand NFL: Making and Selling America's Favorite Sport* (2010); Ken Rappoport's *The Little League That Could: A History of the American Football League* (2010); Neil Leiger's *Guts and Glory: The Golden Age of American Football* (2011); Richard Crepeau's *NFL Football: A History of America's New National Pastime* (2014); and Rob Fleder's *NFL 100: A Century of Pro Football* (2019).

Many of the early games were runaways, or decided by ten or more points—earning it the name "Super Bore," but more recently they have been closer, even nail-biters. Spectators and at-home viewers alike agree that there have been some especially memorable Games, and Seth Trachtman has amassed a list of "The best Super Bowl moments" for Yardbarker.com (February 6, 2021) that you might want to check, but I also welcome your picks. While there are certainly numerous cases of last-minute catches and touchdowns, field goals missed and field goals made, here is my idea of highlights:

- When quarterback "Broadway" Joe Namath boasted a prediction that his New York Jets would beat the highly favored Baltimore Colts in Super Bowl 111/1969 and it actually happened just that way, it was an upset that remains talked about to this day (see Birle 2015).
- Ten years later, at Super Bowl X111/1979, when the Pittsburgh Steelers had a rematch with the Dallas Cowboys, wondering if they could repeat their victory from three years earlier, there was high drama before they became the first three-time champs.
- And another ten years after that, Joe Montana ("Joe Cool") of the San Francisco 49ers again won the MVP award—this time at Super Bowl XX111/1989 with thirty-nine seconds to go in a single clutch shot that ESPN has ranked as the greatest moment in Super Bowl history.
- A single play made all the difference at Super Bowl XXX1V/2000 when defender Mike Jones of the St. Louis Rams grabbed receiver Kevin Dys-

on of the Tennessee Titans, a tackle that kept him just one yard short of the goal line.

- The New England Patriots were the 14-point favorite going into Super Bowl XL11/2008, but Eli Manning of the New York Giants facilitated one of the greatest upsets in NFL history.
- Controversy prevailed at Super Bowl XL1X/2015, New England Patriots vs. the Seattle Seahawks, which was the most-watched show in the US television history, Katy Perry's half-time show the most-watched performance at 118.5M viewers (her "left shark" dancer later identified). Tied at halftime, the tension lasted right up to the end, when the Pats predicted an unusual move by the opposition and won 28-24.
- Brady-Belichick magic continued for Super Bowl L1/2017, and, although dominated by the Atlanta Falcons, the Pats pulled off a comeback for the ages, Tom Brady winning his fifth title (see Holley 2005, 2012). (After he won his seventh title in 2021, with the Tampa Buccaneers, Brady was, at age 43, touted as ageless, a cyborg.)

Super Bowl L11, played in 2018 at the U.S. Bank Stadium in Minneapolis, the Philadelphia Eagles beating the defending champion New England Patriots, holds the record for being the coldest one ever—the temperature at kickoff being only 2°F.

Case Studies from 1991, 2009, and 2021

Encouraging you to check out "Appendix 3: Super Bowl Championships," which includes Roman numeral signifiers, dates, teams and scores, venues, and attendance, there are several contests that stand out, albeit for different reasons. What follows here are case studies from Super Bowl XXV/1991, which took place during the Persian Gulf War; Super Bowl XL111/2009, to demonstrate the role of the host city; and Super Bowl LV/2021, during the COVID-19 pandemic.

Super Bowl XXV/1991

It almost didn't happen. Ten days before what Dave Whalen (2011) described as a "classic contrast in styles: Buffalo's high-octane no-huddle offense against

New York's smashmouth philosophy epitomized by a suffocating defense," the Gulf War had been declared. Both teams, appropriately, had red, white, and blue uniform, and, as they entered the stadium, they were cheered by 74,000 flag-waving fans, many bedecked in "Desert Storm" T-shirts. There were X-ray searches, bomb-sniffing dogs, a newly introduced Gyrocam 360 advanced camera, and antiterrorist squads planted in the stands. The United States, under President George H. W. Bush, had just agreed to combat in what was called "Operation Desert Shield," initiating a massive aerial assault against Saddam Hussein and his Iraqi forces from their neighboring country of Kuwait. The action began just three days before the AFC championship game, and we all wondered whether the game would go on. There was collective relief when Bush announced,

> Life goes on. And this is priority, getting this war concluded properly. But we are not going to screech everything to a halt in terms of our domestic agenda. We're not going to screech everything to a halt in terms of the recreational activities, and I cite the Super Bowl. And I am not going to screech my life to a halt out of some fear about Saddam Hussein. And I think that's a good, clear signal for all Americans to send halfway around the world.

Pre-game pageantry and commentary were replete with patriotism, with viewers introduced, soap-opera style, to some of our soldiers stationed in Saudi Arabia who vowed to watch the game despite its being early morning there. Although it was highly anticipated, no one was quite prepared for the iconic rendition Whitney Houston gave of the national anthem, still held in reverence by those who heard it more than thirty years ago. "And what an image it reinforced," Fuller (1999, 166–167) pointed out, "when people around the world had an opportunity to be led in song by a beautiful, young, talented Black woman in a red, white, and blue outfit." In the midst of comments juxtaposing American priorities, post-kickoff brought pure escapism, the *Los Angeles Times* (Rosenberg 1991) reporting that it affirmed,

> the special place of sports in our culture, whether the Americana-steeped World Series or Madison Avenue-driven Super Bowl. Despite everything occurring on the outside, [it] was its own isolated impregnable world, a seamless, Scudless Saddamless chamber where one could focus on the benign violence of the field without dwelling on the bigger violence looming elsewhere.

Recognizing how many people still recall Super Bowl XXXV/1991, Mia Fischer (2014) reviews it as "a war spectacle involving a barricaded stadium,

X-ray security searches of 72,500 fans, antiterrorist squadrons in the stands, American flags distributed to every seat, an emotional performance of the national anthem by Whitney Houston, and a half-time speech by President George H.W. Bush."

George Rose (Source: Getty Images.)

Super Bowl XL111/2009

"Get your game face on" was the theme for this 43rd Super Bowl, in Tampa, FL, on February 1, 2009, when the Pittsburgh Steelers became the first team to win six Super Bowl championships as it beat the Arizona Cardinals 27-23. Not that the time or place, or frankly even the teams matter much, Patrick Jonsson (2021, 10) reminding us that,

> Success at the Super Bowl is relative. The NFL's national television contracts alone mean that all 32 teams are profitable before the regular season's first downs are even played. And no matter which teams are playing in the Super Bowl, or where it's held, Americans have long ago planned their parties for Sunday.

As host city, Tampa went all out—encouraging residents to "wear a smile Super Bowl week," warmly welcome visitors, and to sport buttons, posters, and point-of-purchase displays about area businesses. Attendees and home viewers alike were treated to Jennifer Hudson singing the National Anthem before the game and Faith Hill doing *God Bless America*, a half-time performance by Bruce

Springsteen and his E Street Band, and a tight thrill up until the end, when the Pittsburgh Steelers (27) stole the championship from the Arizona Cardinals (23) with thirty-five seconds remaining. For the city's fourth time as host, the *Tampa Tribune* suggested five parties one might reasonably attend (Pepsi Smash, ESPN's NEXT Day Tailgate, DirecTV Celebrity, and Bud Bowl), five more "if you have lots of cash" (Gridiron Greats Dinner of Champions, Giving Back Fund's Big Game VIP Event, Saturday Night Spectacular, Inside the Huddle, or Taste of the NFL). Last was a list "You have no hope of attending": The Madden Bowl, the *Maxim* party, ESPN's NEXT VIP Gala, The Commissioner's Party, or (NFL super-agent) Leigh Steinberg's party. Your chances were probably also slim for being invited to Super Bowl parties by Pamela Anderson, Kevin Costner, Snoop Dogg, Jenny McCarthy, or Sean Combs. The Obamas included these elected officials as guests at the President's Super Bowl party: Senators Bob Casey (D-PA), Dick Durbin (D-IL), Amy Klobuchar (D-MN), and Arlen Specter (R-PA), along with Congresspersons Elijah Cummings (D-MD), Artur Davis (D-AL), Rosa DeLauro (D-CT), Charlie Dent (R-PA), Mike Doyle (D-PA), Trent Franks (R-AZ), Raul Grijalva (D-AZ), Hodes (D-NH), Eleanor Holmes-Norton (D-DC), Patrick Murphy (D-PA), and Fred Upton (R-MI) (Sweet 2009). Martha Stewart's seventy-five guests were treated to Super Bowl party foodstuffs categorized as "Dips, Wings, Nachos"; "Pizza, Chili, Sandwiches, Tacos, Ribs and Burgers"; or "Brownies, Sundaes, Cheesecake and Cookies" (Matchar 2009). Emmy-winning sportscaster Al Michaels, who had gone to or watched every Super Bowl, and who called 2009, answered the question as to why we get in a near-holiday mood every year: "Because it happens in winter on a Sunday, when it's cold and getting dark. People are home to watch, and they build a party around it…The Super Bowl is the season-ending culmination of a sport that is clearly now in our consciousness" (cited in Brady 2009).

Super Bowl LV/2021

This most recent Super Bowl, which took place February 7th at the 65,618-capacity Raymond James Stadium in Tampa, FL, will long be remembered as the weirdest, taking place in the thick of the COVID-19/coronavirus pandemic. For our purposes, it best exemplifies the notion that the parties and commercials and half-time show really are the event, not necessarily the sport.

With worries about its possibility of being a superspreader, numerous precautions were put in place: Players were tested regularly, only 25,000 ticketed, socially distanced fans (mostly nasal-swabbed and/or vaccinated healthcare workers, guests of the NFL) were allowed in the stands and corporate suites, interviews took place via videoconferencing rather than in-person, credentialed media numbers were half of last year, and personal protective equipment (PPE) kits with hand sanitizer and a KN95 mask were supplied. Cardboard cutouts were placed around to give the appearance of a packed crowd, but still, everything seemed out of orbit. A study from the University of Mississippi in April 2021 looking at 269 NFL games, 117 with fans, and 152 unattended that found COVID-19 infection rates in fact surged during the second and third weeks from games permitting more than 5,000 fans. There had been many concerns about the pandemic and Super Bowl LV/2021, but, attendance-wise, it came through at #11, with a viewership of 100,466,000; though the lowest audience in fifteen years, it still had sold-out commercial time.

CBS, which charged $5.5M for thirty seconds of ad time, had various streaming platforms, along with NFL and Yahoo! Sports apps, 50 square meters of LED walls, twenty-five cameras, and the movable two-point Flycam. There were more than seven hours of pre-game programming, at three different locales, including a Kickoff show, four and half hour NFL Sunday show, and then the game itself starting at 6:30 p.m. Eastern Standard Time. Thoughts of the pandemic hung over everything—already killing 2M worldwide, 450,000 Americans—so several standard advertisers like Coca-Cola, Hyundai, and Budweiser decided to hold out this year. Uber tried for light humor by bringing back a form of *Wayne's World*, and several firms donated budgets to the Ad Council to fight vaccine skepticism. Some ads addressed the tough times head-on, while others took advantage of us as captive audience. "You may be feeling a little cooped up," Bass Pro Shops intoned, reminding us of better days ahead out in nature. DoorDash made ordering so seem so simple. The social news aggregator Reddit's five-second ad—what looked like two cars racing across a desert, then merging to become the company's symbol; it flitted so quickly that many viewers may have only gotten it subconsciously, but the spot became the most-discussed one of the day.

The Old Boy's Club was broken a bit as this Fifty-Fifth Super Bowl was officiated by a woman (Sarah Thomas) for the first time in its history and female coaches Lori Locust (defensive line assistant) and Maral Javadifar (assistant strength and conditioning coach) were part of the Buccaneers' staff, along with Carly Helfand as scouting assistant and Jackie Davidson directing football research. Julie Frymyer and Tiffany Morton served as assistant athletic trainers for the Chiefs. Still, it was noticeable that the NFL has done nothing about sensitivity to the Chief's "tomahawk chop" that many find disrespectful to our First People, Colin Kaepernick's name never came up in the broadcast, and much remains to be done toward advancing Black coaches (like the Chief's offensive coordinator Eric Bieniemy). "The NFL espoused racial unity and praised health care workers. But its inaction on racial diversity, its stereotypic imagery and its decision to host a potential superspreader event said something different," noted Ken Belson (2021). In so many ways this was one for the history books.

Oh—the Tampa Bay Buccaneers beat the Kansas City Chiefs 31-9, quarterback Tom Brady winning his seventh Lombardi Trophy, if the first with the Bucs, and his universally being declared as "ageless." Miley Cyrus headlined the TikTok Tailgate concert, Jazmine Sullivan and Eric Church did a duet of the national anthem, H.E.R did *America the Beautiful*, National Youth Poet Laureate Amanda Gorman recited an original poem, and Canadian singer The Weeknd starred at halftime—from the stands. The ratings were the lowest since 2007, at 96.4M viewers, but it hardly mattered as what will be thought of as the pandemic Super Bowl still was one of the most-watched television shows during a lockdown when television was at an all-time high as an essential source of infotainment.

Historical Perspective

The Super Bowl is quintessentially contemporary in its mustering of the latest communications technologies and showcasing of the latest consumer products. Conversely, it is also downright ancient in the way it valorizes violent combat, valorous combatants, territorial conquest, and cultural conformity. Though Superman, superhighways, supermarkets, supersonic transport and other superlatives existed prior to the first Super Bowl in 1966, the cultural work of the Super Bowl is an influential precursor to the era of super sizing.

—Michael Mooradian Lupro, "The Super in the Super Bowl." (2013, 93)

Along with the celebrations, of course, have come complications. "There may be no greater cruelty in modern sports than the toll pro football has taken on the bodies and brains of its players," Kevin Cook (2012, xii) has posited. While this book outlines issues surrounding the Super Bowl, including the dark sides of gambling, sexism, racism, and the violence factor, it only tangentially touches on nastier concerns such as sex, drugs, and alcohol, or the big one of concussions. Consider: Jerry Green, the only sportswriter who covered the first fifty-five Super Bowls (1967–2021), called it "an annual slopfest in the dungeon of excess" (1991). Many of these topics are covered widely elsewhere, and need to be researched and respected, but my aim is to keep it all in perspective. So, moving on from this very brief historical review of the Game(s), party on as you read about its ecopolitics and sociocultural aspects.

## CHAPTER 3

Ecopolitics of the Super Bowl

The Super Bowl is used by CEOs "as a vehicle to cement deals, entertain clients, reward productive employees with a free excursion, and simultaneously create tax deductions."

—Dona Schwartz, *Contesting the Super Bowl* (1997, 2)

This quotation from nearly a quarter-century ago still holds, Super Sunday being not only our biggest sporting event but also one of our biggest money-making ones. The NFL signed new media rights agreements with CBS, ESPN, Fox, NBC, and Amazon in 2021 worth $110B as player salaries continued to escalate. Host cities for the Super Bowl are encouraged to expect to bring in $300+M (Queenan 2009), with many tax subsidies provided for the NFL, and, while gamblers might earn staggering amounts off the results, individual players earn enormous bonuses (and rings, with 250+ diamonds, costing $10,000+) just for participating. By the time it turned 100, in 2019, *Forbes* determined that the average NFL franchise was worth $2.86B—a six-fold increase in the last two decades. The Independent Evaluation Group (IEG)/World Bank Group found NFL sponsorship revenue defied COVID-19 to reach $1.62B in 2020, with income from gambling up around 25 percent. "As a nonprofit, it earns more than the Y, the Red Cross, Goodwill, the Salvation Army or Catholic Charities—yet it stands as one of the greatest profit-generating commercial advertising, entertainment and media enterprises ever created," Tom Watson (2014) explains. "An arcane tax code change that eased the 1966 merger of the NFL with the old AFL landed the new combined entity in section 501(c)6 of the tax code, designated as an industry association." Eric Reed (2020) points out the NFL's many sources of revenue—tens of millions from merchandising, branded partnerships, ticket sales, network broadcasting, ad sales, local revenues, and even international sales of merchandise. Basically, the professionals surrounding Super Bowl own us for a week, fulfilling football junkies' fondest wishes.

"America loves football, from Turkey Day touch to Friday Night Lights, from State U. Saturdays to the NFL," David Von Drehl (2014) has declared.

"And with love comes indulgence, a tolerance for ignoring the rules that govern the rest of us. The National Football League has been exempted from antitrust laws, shielded from tax collectors, fattened by television moguls bearing billion-dollar contracts." In 2015, however, the league lost its tax-exempt status after intense criticism, and, although it no longer is required to publicly disclose its tax return, it appears on track to fulfill its commissioner's goal of revenue of $25B by 2027.

Planning and profits relative to advertising, merchandising, tourism, security, and all those parties are all organized well in advance of the games. Demand for insanely high-priced tickets still far exceeds their provision—only about 1 percent being available to the general public, through a random drawing. According to sportingnews.com, the cheapest tickets for Super Bowl LV/2021 were $4,313 for Vivid Seats, $4,025 through StubHub, and $4,950 NFL Exchange; although the official website said that pricing started at $5,950, Ticketmaster was selling some for as high as $40,000 the Friday before the game (El-Bawab 2021). (Do you see now why I called them insanely high prices, and why I despair about how many working-class fans can, or even should, afford them?). Meanwhile, some 100M of the rest of us watch on televisions or streaming services—oblivious to the fact that WE are the ones actually being sold, to advertisers, for ever-increasing prices.

"Our sports culture shapes societal attitudes, relationships, and power arrangements," esteemed sportswriter Dave Zirin wrote in 2013 (10), labeling the Super Bowl as "perennially the Woodstock for the one percent" (31). *Forbes* (Reimer 2020) called Super Bowl L1V the most political in history: "[It] captured the mood of the country. It was political, loud, and hysterical. Donald Trump's outlandish presidency loomed over Hard Rock Stadium in Miami on Sunday, from militaristic pre-game festivities to a defiant half-time show involving Latinx superstars Jennifer Lopez and Shakira…corporate social progressivism was on full display." When several dozen winning New England Patriots refused an invitation to the White House for political reasons, it was particularly awkward knowing that their owner, Robert K. Kraft, had contributed $1M to Trump's inaugural festivities. Listen to the verbiage used by Ari Fleischer, press secretary to George W. Bush, in an opinion piece in *Wall Street Journal* December 28, 2017:

> The first quarter of President Trump's term is almost over. To grade his performance in football terms, he deserves credit for moving the ball down the field over several different drives. But he has committed so many unnecessary

roughness penalties, along with giving up one huge fumble, that he may have to gain 200 yards just to score one touchdown.

Mark Leibovich, author of *Big Game: The NFL in Dangerous Times* (2018), has drawn parallels between the two entertainment dynasties, saying both Trump and the NFL fashion, politics, and sport as a reality show. When we met during his book tour, Leibovich emphasized the fact that our fandom will probably save football, and the Super Bowl, in the long run. Just follow the money.

The most recent Super Bowl, predicted to be even more political in light of the January 6th insurrection at the Capitol, cases of police brutality, and the mask issue, turned out to be less about politics and more about hopes for unity—echoing what Butterworth (2008, 310) has suggested: Football as a civil religion united should be "around a set of 'sacred' heroes, documents, and ideals." Maybe there is something to the notion that Super Bowl is, in fact, one of our key enduring trans-partisan events.

In our continual quest for escapism and entertainment, the Super Bowl provides the perfect antidote, but we must realize that it comes with a cost. While we are encouraged to fill cavernous stadiums and to spend time and money while we engorge ourselves watching and/or listening and/or taping the Game, consider who is producing the program, and why. Remembering that we are celebrating a spectacle whereby wealthy elites own and control the $10+B football industry and oftentimes the media that reports on it, this chapter on the ecopolitics of the Super Bowl considers those stakeholders, host cities, commercials, the production of Super Bowl, including pre-game and half-time festivities, gambling, and the role of media in terms of ratings, sportscasters, and social media. It's not called Super for nothing, this Bowl.

Stakeholders

In my world—advertising—the Super Bowl is judgment day. If politicians have Election Day and Hollywood has the Oscars, advertising has the Super Bowl.

—Jerry Della Femina, *Wall Street Journal* (2001)

Get out your calculator, but be aware that no matter how much you might add up relative to how much money is earned by the Super Bowl there are probably still some receipts we will never know about. Memorabilia is an industry unto itself, programs going for $250 to $450, rings valued at $5M for a team, the famous ball at the center of "Deflategate" $43,750, the jersey worn by Jim Brown during the 1962 to 1963 season $78,000 and by Johnny Unitas in 1967 $103,500, and O. J. Simpson's 1968 Heisman Trophy $230,000. That just gets you started. Add annual ticket sales of $60+M, television rights of $3+B, merchandising revenue of $500+M, and you can see how it all translates into dollar signs. Most amazing, though, is the fact that that the NFL also got about $1B in the form of state and federal subsidies because it was deemed a nonprofit (Steele 2014)—although the league itself gave up its nonprofit status the next year. Individual teams have enormous value, Taylor (2019) divulging these stats on the world's most value sports franchises: Dallas Cowboys $5.7B, New England Patriots $4.4B, New York Giants $4.3B, the Washington Football Team $3.5B, San Francisco 49ers $3.8B, Los Angeles Rams $4B, and Chicago Bears $3.5B. Small wonder that Hopsicker and Dyreson (2017) deem the NFL to be "the most influential and lucrative entertainment behemoth in the national landscape, a multi-billion dollar industrial giant that dominates US television broadcasting and aspires to global mega-event status." From the start it has been watched by neighboring Canada and Mexico, beamed to our armed forces in foreign outposts, and now viewed in Europe, Asia, and Australia. Word is that it is watched worldwide in more than 130 countries, in more than thirty languages. Fox claims that the global audience numbers around 1B.

Continually becoming a corporate tool, where tents and hospitality suites, private planes and bashes prevail, Super Bowl essentially is a soup bowl soliciting contributions. The City of Tampa, for the Thirty-Fifth Super Bowl, in 2001, included The Playboy Party, The Penthouse Party, and The Maxim Party along with celebrity parties, the Player's Super Bowl Tailgate, the Leather and Lace Party, and many more. Most were invitation-only, just as evites are sent out today.

The most prominent player in the NFL is its longtime serving commissioner, Roger Goodell, chosen in 2006 to succeed Paul Tagliabue. Patrick Pinak (2021) reminds us that

> The 61-year-old has been criticized for his handling of things like the Colin Kaepernick national anthem fiasco, the league's domestic violence policy regarding players like Ray Rice, the severity of penalties imposed on Saints coaches and players involved in Bountygate and the New England Patriots, Tom Brady and the Spygate and Deflategate scandals.

Yet, ESPN Stats & Info reports that Goodell has made more than $200M since 2006 in his role as NFL Commissioner.

If you, a simple fan, want to attend a Super Bowl, you better start saving your money. The starting price for tickets is $5,950, parking ranges from $120 to $360, and other extraneous items such as food and drink, lodging, souvenirs, and airfare all add up. In 2014, Josh Finkelman of New Jersey was so upset with how already expensive tickets became out of reach, he launched a class action lawsuit questioning how a face value ticket of $500 could quadruple or more in cost, but five years later the state Supreme Court ruled that the NFL did not violate consumer fraud law, as 1 percent of Super Bowl tickets were available through a lottery. Employers in host cities, who typically lose around $3B in productivity due to the number of workers who call in sick the day after, should also be factored in as stakeholders. Without even counting the number of people who leave work to go to the games, estimates are that 10.5M take the day off ahead of time, 6M cancel that day, and some 7.5M will come in late to work.

Host Cities

> The Super Bowl attracts more viewers and creates more revenue than any other single sport event. The Super Bowl, however, is more than just a game to the National Football League (NFL) and the communities that host it. Increasingly, organizing (host) committees, nonprofit organizations, and local governments in cities that are awarded the game use the event as a catalyst to address pressing social issues.
> —Babiak and Wolfe, "More Than Just a Game?" (2006, 214)

Bending to notions of corporate social responsibility, the NFL is acutely aware of its public image, especially relative to the various cities. For our purposes, this statement on its website has particular relevance: "As part of each Super Bowl's community investment, the NFL works with local organizations to develop programs focusing on youth outreach, health and wellness, the arts, education, business advancement for racial and gender minorities, and community rebuilding." It might surprise some fans to know the extent to which the NFL has taken this commitment and how many initiatives it has implemented in the host cities of its crowning event. Horrow and Swatek (2011) outline the baseline hosting requirements:

- At least 19,000 hotel rooms that require three- or four-night minimum stays, including rooms for both teams and NFL personnel;
- A 70,000-seat stadium or one that can be expanded to at least that size;

- A range of nearby facilities or spaces to house the media and accreditation center for more than 4,000 media representatives, the NFL Experience, the NFL Tailgate Party, and the like;
- An average daily temperature of 50°F (10°C) or above the week of the game, or a climate-controlled indoor facility;
- Provision of police, fire, ambulance, and other infrastructure services at no cost to the NFL.

As you can see on "Appendix 6: Super Bowl Host Cites," Miami holds the record for hosting the most Games (11), Arizona four times, and will again in 2023 through a process whereby the NFL identified and negotiated the site rather than using a bidding process—a first, if a third time the University of Phoenix Stadium will be used. New Orleans is already preparing for LVIII/2024. When a host committee found that Super Bowl LV/2021 generated an economic impact of $720M for the local economy, the thought was that by 2023 that number could reach or even exceed $1B. For foodies, though, the even happier news is that Tucson's famous Jalapeño Poppers will be available—sliced and filled with a rich creamy cheese mixture, topped with Panko and baked until bubbly; small wonder they have become a Super Bowl obsession.

The experiences various cities have of course differed depending on the times, Houston's ranging from humdrum to finding a "morality clause" at its old Astrodome to being supersized. Phoenix learned a lesson when it voted not to make Martin Luther King Jr. Day to be a paid holiday and lost Super Bowl XXVII/1993 but bemoans the city's sports debt. San Francisco welcomes all those partying spenders but still feels cursed that its 49ers held to history by losing on home turf for Super Bowl 50/2016. Miami, the record-holder, uses the games to showcase local artists, activities, and food from Calle Ocho sausages to Stone crabs.

When Super Bowl XLVI/2012 was being played at Lucas Oil Stadium in Indianapolis, Giants defeating the Patriots, Indiana hospitality was on full display for its first time as host. "A nationwide army of knitters, crocheters and weavers…Thousands of scarf-makers, from great-grandmothers to prison inmates" came together to make more than 13,000 blue and white scarves for volunteers to stay both warm and visible, the AP (Callahan 2012) reported. While the designs varied from simple stripes to those with intricate Super Bowl–related themes, the project was so successful that extra scarves were sent to Belgium, Canada, South Africa, and the UK. For Super Bowl 50/2016, the host committee recruited 5,000 volunteers as greeters, 500 more to set up the stage for halftime, but the part you will really enjoy is Gabriel Thompson's 2016 *Slate* article, about being a Super Bowl concession worker: "What it's like making less than $13 an hour to serve $13 beers at one of the biggest games on Earth."

Reporting on Super Bowl LIV/2020, *Miami Today* (Henseler 2020), the host committee found that "the Super Bowl and surrounding events brought 4,597 full- and part-time jobs to South Florida and had a total economic impact of $571.9M…Visitor spending by spectators, media, teams and NFL staff made up $246M of the total impact, while event hosting by the NFL and Miami Dolphins added $325.8M." Hotel rates were boosted by about three times their usual cost, and a survey showed that the average spectator had spent $1,781/day and the average media member $2,154/day. Just as importantly, as attendees are concerned about the possibility of terrorism at mega-events, Miller, Veltri, and Gillentine (2008) encourage us relative to proactive steps toward Super Bowls offering a "reasonably safe environment."

Commercials

> The National Football League's Super Bowl is not just the crowning glory of American football. It is the Super Bowl of advertising, the most watched, most anticipated, most expensive, most influential arena for major-league television advertising. For corporate America, the real event starts when an advertiser makes its pitch for a piece of your wallet.
>
> —Bernice Kanner, *The Super Bowl of Advertising* (2004, 1)

Probably one of the first ads that caught the public attention was when blonde bombshell Farrah Fawcett seductively lathered Noxzema shaving cream all over New York Jets quarterback "Broadway" Joe Namath's face. The thirty-second spot for Super Bowl VII/1973 may have cost $42,000, but it set a stage that no one would have predicted.

When the Pittsburgh Steelers' Mean Joe Greene tossed his Coca-Cola and yelled "Hey Kid, Catch!" at Super Bowl X1V/1980, the whole world seemed to have caught it, and, like many other commercials, it has become subsumed into our vocabularies. Four years later, Apple's "1984" ad is widely considered the most famous, though; based on George Orwell's novel, it introduced the Macintosh computer to a national audience. *Forbes* (Hanlon 2014) describes it as winning the Game:

The commercial showed the future in a monochromatic hyper industrial gray. Uniformly expressionless humans are assembled before a giant screen as big brother delivers a monotone about "the great body of the state" and "the unification of thought." In the midst of all the dread, a young blonde woman (a model and former discus thrower Anya Major) wearing red shorts and a white Apple Macintosh t-shirt sprints through the assembled storm troopers and human drones to fling a sledgehammer at the screen. Over the sudden blast of glare, an announcer intones,

—"On January 24th, Apple Computer will introduce Macintosh. And you'll see why 1984 won't be like '1984.' "

The general consensus is that, after Apple's dramatic launch of the Macintosh computer in 1984, consumers expect to learn about new products and actually anticipate enjoying the infotainment.

Since 1989, the USA Today Super Bowl Ad Meter, with an online element added in 2013, Anheuser-Busch being the biggest overall winner, followed by PepsiCo, Hyundai, and Nike. While there have been many memorable ones, you might think of Jerry Seinfeld and an animated Superman in the 1998 AMEX ad, Brad Pitt drinking Heineken in a 2005 commercial while being harassed by paparazzi, Cindy Crawford in a white swimsuit drinking Pepsi as she stepped out of a red Lamborghini in 1992, Budweiser's monosyllabic frogs of 1995, Old Spice's 2010 "The man your man could smell…," the e-Trade talking baby (2008–2013), 88-year-old Betty White being tackled into a mud pile, then eating a Snickers bar, and so many more that you can probably cite. Super Bowl XXX1V/2000 was so crammed with internet-related companies that it was dubbed the "dot-com Super Bowl." "Not only are the commercials aired during the broadcast specifically produced for, and premiered at this event, they are the subject of intense media interest in themselves and widespread reporting on their costs, tables of the most popular ads and so on," O'Donnell and Spires (2008, 2) remind us.

Overwhelmingly aimed at affluence, they tend to include enticements for fancy cars, fun-loving lifestyles, masculine fantasies and drugs to help get them there, technological gadgets, and credit cards on which to put (off) the expenses. There have also been questionable ads relative to cultural appropriation, pro-life, dating services, politics, suicide, immigration, raunchiness, and a select few that might have difficulty in translation to other countries or cultures.

Building on the popularity of the games, it has become something of a cliché, as Matthew P. McAllister (2003) has pointed out, to say that some people—

supposedly one in ten, watch just for the commercials: "The news media play up the hype of Super Bowl advertising with pregame anticipatory stories and postgame analyses focusing on the commercials." Networks and water cooler gatherers discuss them the next day, social media vote for the best and the worst, and entire television shows are devoted to the topic. The actual game is often considered a sidebar to the commercials that drive it, and this small section devoted to them clearly is just an introduction to their importance both economically and socioculturally.

Considered cutting-edge and clever, Super Bowl ads and promos for upcoming shows often use women as the butt (no pun intended) of many jokes, whether by innuendo or simple gross-out. "The upshot," according to Lisa Bennett (2003, 1), NOW Foundations Communications Director who performed a content analysis of Super Sunday 2003: "These commercials were designed to entertain particularly immature boys and men addicted to the sex-violence métier of video games, who also think scatological joking around is hilarious." Cartoons and violence also rule among advertisers, according to Bruce Venden Bergh, professor of advertising at Michigan State University (Sutel 2006). "The role of women in the discursive formation generated by and around the Super Bowl could be defined as the obligation to look good, to provide (often unseen) moral support and to give birth to future generations of Americans," note O'Donnell and Spires (2008). They expand this notion by declaring that women's presence at Super Bowls are limited to cheerleaders, the occasional sideline reporter, or players' wives; "In the adverts women appear wither as sexy adjuncts for men, as distractions from more properly 'manly business, or they provide an unseen moral structure to men's lives." Still, as Deborah Yao (2009) phrases it, "The Super Bowl remains the premier advertising event." It has even been considered the ultimate corporate advertising event, disguised as a game.

Besides those who actually advertise on Super Sunday, a number of other companies do so tangentially. Glad trash bags suggested their use for you to "Get Ready for the Big Game"; Ex-Lax promoted "YOUR TEAM FOR RELIEF: Tackle Discomfort with the Brands You Trust," Prilosec features (supposed) user Brett Favre with the statement "It's time to GET TOUGH on heartburn"; King Oscar sardines promote their product with, "For your health, this is a touchdown"; Blue Diamond as "The Football Nut"; Frigidaire as "Your starting lineup"; and New! Chewable (Maalox) configured its visuals in a football frame featuring "Gas-X."

All the talk the day after Super Bowl XL111/2019 was about how the winning ad came from amateurs. Scoring higher than Bud or Bridgestone (tires),

Pedigree or Pepsi, Cars.com or Castrol, brothers Dave and Joe Herbert's "Free Doritos" has a guy shatter a vending machine with his crystal ball after it made a prediction the chips would be free to everyone in an office. "And it could be a game-changer," decided Bruce Horovitz (2009, 4B). "For the first time, it wasn't an ad agency that created the best-liked Super Bowl commercial." Their prize for winning Frito-Lay's online contest: $1M. The truly amazing part of Super Bowl advertising is that, as McAllister and Galindo-Ramirez (2017) point out, its "spectacular nature" has given birth to subsets such as the decades-long Doritos user-generated contests, *Greatest Super Bowl Commercials* television specials, and branded entertainment as part of the celebration. In 2016, its "Crash the Super Bowl" website asked people to pick their favorite consumer-generated ad, "Ultrasound," where a fetus has premature cravings for Nacho Cheese winning, and in 2019 Lil Nas X and Sam Elliott had a Doritos dance-off at the "Cool Ranch."

Super Bowl XXXIX/2005 experimented with product placement—having players drink Pepsi, douse themselves in Axe Deodorant Bodyspray for Men, drive Fords, use H&R Block or Verizon, but it was haphazard and not well received. Jan Huebenthal (2013, 44) offers an interesting deep reading of a 2007 Snickers candy bar commercial:

> Two mechanics, clad in blue-collar uniforms, unshaven, and rough-looking, are working on a car motor when one of the two men pulls out a Snickers bar and starts eating it. The other man is immediately mesmerized by the chocolate bar, biting into it from the other side. As the two men hungrily devour the Snickers bar, each from a different side, their lips meet. After a second of paralyzing shock, they hastily pull away from each other.
> Mechanic I: "I think we just accidentally kissed!"
> Mechanic II: "Quick! Do something manly!"
> Both men tear out a chunk of their chest hair, screaming in agony.
> Tagline: "Snickers. Most Satisfying."

Saying that it "exemplifies promotional culture conflating male homosexuality with femininity, and then rendering this conflation as a source of emasculation," Huebenthal points out that the ad drew protests from gay organizations, and it ultimately was withdrawn. So much for notions of homophobic humor and how different people "read" advertisements differently. A decade later, Super Bowl LI/2017 gave an unintended boost to Kellogg when an older ad for Eggo waffles was aired on YouTube as part of Netflix's *Stranger Things* program—a point that Ribbonworks Lanyards made in its own interest plugging products like wristbands and sweatbands. Gillette's "Be a man" ad—seen by *Christian Science*

Monitor (Bruinius 2019) as a collage of toxic masculinity for subjects such as the #MeToo movement and holding men responsible—had its share of controversy but generally was well received. And apparently the man who made sure his Vodka Mule was seen while H.E.R. sang at Super Bowl LV/2021 must be happy, as the image went viral (see #superbowl2021#productplacement#VodkaMule).

As commercials reflect their times, during Super Bowl L1/2017, in the thick of polarization over topics such as a border wall against immigrants, it was striking that Bud aired an ad featuring its founder, Adolphus Busch, *New Yorker* (Crouch 2017) remarking,

> Arriving as it did, on the heels of a tumultuous week—after the Trump Administration issued a travel ban on all refugees and on visa holders from seven Muslim-majority countries, and an outraged portion of the country rose up against it—the ad was interpreted as making a clear political statement…Despite what Budweiser wants us to believe, beer is not bipartisan.

Coke had a multiracial cast belt out *America the Beautiful*, eighty-four Lumber profiled mother–daughter migrants coming from Mexico, and Airbnb aired a spot challenging the notion of a travel ban. Or consider how Mr. Peanut was supposed to die during Super Bowl L1V/2020, but Planters retracted the story in light of Kobe Bryant's death and the anthropomorphized nut is still with us. "Appendix 7: Super Bowl Costs for 30-Second Commercials" gives the best picture. "In the short span of a half century," Crepeau (2017) notes about Super Bowl 50, what began as a modest championship match between two football leagues has grown into a "outsized mid-winter holiday"—from a one-day to a two-week festival. Marketing and media "have aided and abetted the growth of this celebration of football and consumption." For 2016, Ember pointed out how advertisers deployed well-worn playbooks: "A combination of humor, celebrities and plenty of animals," along with some seriously scripted messages such as No More (to combat sexual assault), Colgate's spot to encourage people to save water while brushing their teeth, Helen Mirren urging people not to drive drunk. Falling as it does in the post-holiday season that has a gap until Valentine's Day, the timing of the game is a marketer's dream. Humor is gender- and culture-dependent (Duncan and Aycock 2008), celebrityhood is time- and place-dependent, and anyone knows that animals as actors are iffy at best.

Audiences for the Super Bowl are enormous, there are literally thousands of products, and the buzz is built in. Consider: for a platform able to reach half of the United States simultaneously, small wonder that so much media has been devoted to this topic, that many young people can cite ads that aired before they were born, and that the prices just keep climbing. Convergence culture theorist Henry Jenkins (2006, 87) has said that the Super Bowl has become "a showcase for advertising as a sporting event"; no one would argue that its commercials have become a cultural phenomenon unto themselves.

Production, Including Pre-Game and Half-Time Festivities

Pre-Game

Months, weeks, days, and hours before the actual game build to a frenzy still preceded by introductions to the teams, Pledge of Allegiance, the national anthem (the general consensus being that Whitney Houston's 1991 rendition was the best), and then a coin toss to see which team will kick off and which will receive. It should be noted that, since 1992, American Sign Language is used alongside lead singers, available on the stadium's Jumbotron.

Half-Time Shows

[The Super Bowl half-time show] is by definition the biggest stage in music…a coronation for the artists who perform.

—Daniel D'Addario, "At the Super Bowl, Justin Timberlake Plays a High-Stakes Game." (2018)

A tradition drawing almost as much attention as the game itself, Super Bowl's half-time shows range from the reason some people tune in at all to being highly anticipated pop cultural barometers. Many draw on nostalgic themes and most become bellwethers for the host television network to promote their upcoming programs. For those who have only been noshing on items like Buffalo Cauliflower Dip with chips and beer, it offers a time to sit and do some serious eating, while for the dance crowd the half-time show is a perfect time to let off steam.

It has been seventeen years now, but when people talk about half-time shows, Super Bowl XXXVIII/2004 is right up there as a time capsule. Known as "Nipplegate," the shocking event was that, as Janet Jackson and Justin Timberlake were performing, there was a "wardrobe malfunction" such that a nipple shield in Jackson's bustier became exposed for nine sixteenths of a second before 150M viewers. You would have thought that it was a much longer exposure from the reaction, as the FCC issued CBS fines of $550,000 and campaigned again "indecent" broadcasting, the NFL declared that MTV would no longer be allowed to produce half-time shows, and Jackson's music was blacklisted. Was Nipplegate symbolic of declining morality, or was it simply a publicity stunt? Lawrence A. Wenner (2008) has written about how the "moral contagion" following the brief breast exposure eventually cooled, Feeney (2014) discusses the cultural and political legacy a decade later, "Janet Jackson" became the most searched term/event in internet history, and an entire industry emerged relative to video sharing, Facebook being launched three days later. In an era of awareness of "shaming," it seems appropriate that Justin Timberlake only recently publicly apologized for what had become known as "The Janet Jackson" scandal. November 2021 was when FX and Hulu released the documentary *Malfunction: The Dressing Down of Janet Jackson*, showing how her career from CBS' Les Moonves and throughout the entertainment industry was kept on hold while Timberlake's soared, including another half-time performance for him at Super Bowl L11/2018. Timberlake's *Mea Culpa*, which included a nod to Britney Spears, went like this:

> I am deeply sorry for the times in my life where my actions have contributed to the problem, where I spoke out of turn, or did not speak up for what was right. I understand that I fell short in these moments and in many others and benefited a system that condones misogyny and racism.

Frank Micelotta (Source: Getty Images)

"The Super Bowl Halftime Show wasn't always the extravaganza it is today," Matt Doeden (2017, 50) informs us. "At first, halftime was an afterthought, often featuring marching bands from local universities to entertain the fans while the players nursed their bruises." Those early half-time shows were basically musical spectacles, "wholesome" performances consisting of college marching bands, drill teams, and ensemble groups like *Up with People*, but once producers realized what a bonanza they had, it became a draw onto itself. The first celebrity per se to perform at halftime was Carol Channing, star of *Hello, Dolly!* at Super Bowl 1V/1970, and then it took several decades before the value of that time slot was realized. One might credit the boy band New Kids on the Block at Super Bowl XXV/1991, Gloria Estefan in 1992, and then came Michael Jackson's blockbuster performance in 1993 that put Super Bowl halftime on an entirely new celebrity-oriented course. Here is that A-list, chronologically: country music singers Clint Black, Tanya Tucker, Travis Tritt, and the Judds 1994; Patti Labelle 1995; Diana Ross 1996; Blues Brothers 1997; Boys 11 Men, Smokey Robinson, Martha Reeves, The Temptations, and Queen Latifah 1998; Gloria Estefan and Stevie Wonder 1999; Phil Collins, Christina Aguilera, Toni Braxton and an 80-person choir with Edward James Olmos 2000; Aerosmith, Britney Spears, Mary J. Blige, and Nelly 2001; U2 2002; Shania Twain 2003; Jessica Simpson, P. Diddy, Nelly, Kid Rock, Janet Jackson and Justin Timberlake 2004; Paul McCartney 2005; The Rolling Stones 2006; Prince 2007; Tom Petty and the Heartbreakers 2008; Bruce Springsteen 2009; The Who 2010; The Black Eyed Peas with Usher and Slash 2011; Madonna 2012; *Beyoncé* 2013; Bruno Mars 2014; Katy Perry 2015 (the most-watched TV half-time show, with 118.5M viewers); Coldplay 2016; Lady Gaga 2017; Justin Timberlake 2018; Maroon 5 2019; Shakira and Jennifer Lopez 2020 (the most-watched half-time show on YouTube, with strong Latinx statements sent to 195M viewers); and The Weeknd 2021.

In 2022, J. Lo's documentary *Halftime* was released opening night at the Tribeca Film Festival; directed by Amanda Micheli, it follows her career while focusing on her performance at Super Bowl L1V. For the film, Lopez rerecorded an orchestral version of *Same Girl (Halftime Remix)* as well as *This Land Is Your Land* in coordination with its release, featuring a cast that included her soon-to-be husband Ben Affleck along with Shakira, Julia Stiles, Constance Wu, and a number of well-known musicians and artistic producers. While more an intimate portrait of J. Lo the superstar than an eye-opener into that 2020 performance, it does chronicle her rehearsing for it, and, overall, it is a rare opportunity to see a woman juggling work and family amidst global attention.

As you skim the overall list of Who's Who of pop music, small wonder that being chosen as a half-time performer is a status within itself. Therefore, when artists Rihanna, Cardi B, and Jay-Z declined for Super Bowl L111/2019 in support of Colin Kaepernick, it was quite a statement. Torn between a civil debate and civil rights, the white-boy soul group Maroon 5 performed despite an online petition of 110,000+ signatures but joined with the NFL and Interscope Records to make a $500,000 donation to Big Brothers Big Sisters of America. A topic worthy of a book unto itself, halftime is rife with issues of cultural diversity, body image, athleticism, patriotism, performance, and more, but at least the hope is that you will be doing your own decoding. For Super Bowl LV11/2023, Rihanna changed her allegiance, agreeing to perform at halftime as her first public appearance since the Grammy Awards of 2018. Even bigger than that, though, was the news that Apple Music will sponsor the show—a deal the NFL had been seeking, with a promise of as much as $2.5B for rights to NFL Sunday Ticket.

Counterprogramming

Counterprogramming to the Super Bowl has been attempted since 1992, when Fox, which had tried *Up with People*, broadcast a live edition of *In Living Color*, with Gloria Estefan, at halftime that drew 22M viewers, but the alternative only encouraged producers to expand and fancify their broadcast offerings. MTV had enough success with *Beavis and Butt-Head* that it ran from 1994 to 1999 during the Games, Celebrity Deathmatch in 1988 and 1999, *WWF Sunday Night Heat* played in 1999 and 2000 on the USA channel, and NBC introduced a Playboy Playmates edition to its *Fear Factor* in 2002 that drew 11.4M viewers.

Pay-per-view took note, and the X League women's tackle team, scantily clad, started in 2004, eventually becoming the Lingerie Football League in 2009 then rebranding again in 2013 as the Legends Football League. Based on the strategy that "sex sells," the *Lingerie Bowl* featured women wearing helmets, shoulder, elbow and knee pads, and bras and underwear as they played full-contact seven-on-seven football. At their first competition, Team Dream beat Team Euphoria 6-0, but the real winners were the advertisers for an audience of 40M viewers. Extended to Canada and Australia, called the "ultimate fantasy football game," it announced Mike Ditka as its chair in

2020 and decided to call itself The Extreme Football League. If garters and lace from shoulder pads were removed, its outfits still are sexy—the thinking being that tackling is easier when the opponent isn't hampered by too much clothing. Kasie Murphy gathered stories from ten former players in 2020, finding symbolic violence (accepted structural levels of control) in three areas: denial of resources (low pay), inferior treatment (treated like a sex symbol), and a limitation of aspirations. "It's the only professional women's league that gets attention…sometimes when you're a female athlete you have to suck it up. You have to do whatever it takes to get people to your games," are some of the refrains she heard.

In 2014, the *Kitten Bowl* was attempted by the Hallmark Channel—the lol-cats and the Aristocats, television personality Beth Stern hosting the rescue pet adoption process at #kittenbowl. As the competitors claw their way to victory, the winning news is that some 50,000 shelter pets have found homes. The Houston Humane Society sponsored a Kitten Bowl Tailgate Party in 2021 over "Su-purr Bowl weekend," offering furry friends that were neutered, micro-chipped, and vaccinated—ready for "play-by-play kitten action." Also in 2014, Nat Geo introduced the Fish Bowl, the Los Angeles Clams vs. the Buffalo Gills three years later—"anyfin" being possible. "We created a fake fish football championship that is destined to be playing in the background while thousands of Super Bowl party hosts prep for the main event," said the general manager of Nat Geo WILD. "That's right, rip open the chips, put out the guacamole, and prep your Jell-O shots while your cat goes crazy watching the biggest night in aquatic sports history."

Animal Planet, however, has had the biggest hit with the *Puppy Bowl*, which started in 2005. Featuring puppies from shelters—ostensibly to raise awareness about adopting/rescuing abandoned dogs, it continues to be quite a "pup-ular" ratings hit. Monitored by a veterinarian and representatives of the American Society for the Prevention of Cruelty to Animals (ASPCA) and animal shelters, the pre-taped show is shot by 25+ cameras in a no-au-dience stadium to some 10+M viewers who see Team Ruff compete against Team Fluff, the plexiglass coated with peanut butter so that the cuties can lick it for viewers to see what fun they were having. Human "rufferees" check the action while announcers call out touchdowns, timeouts, and pen-alties, using epithets such as "illegal bathing" for playing in the water bowl, "premature watering of the lawn" for urinating, "excessive fertilization" for pooping. An MVP (Most Valuable Puppy) is chosen. Aware of political correctness, special needs dogs have been included, chickens have been used as cheerleaders, and, appropriately, skunks have served as referees. Not necessarily meant as a political statement, people still talk about how Mabel, a 1-year-old Jack Russell, had a bowel movement during the playing of the national anthem at Puppy Bowl 2017. Early shows drew audiences of 7+M viewers, but those numbers have continued to grow over the years, along with advertising revenues and host celebrities such as Martha Stewart and Snoop Dogg—making it nearly "pawfect." Puppy Parties are popular, encouraging invitees to bring their own canines and to vote for who should win the chewy trophy.

Post-Game

For those who think the Super Bowl is endless, there is an element of truth there. Networks vie to air it so that they can insert what is known as "coattail" programming of their other offerings. So, in addition to extensive reviewing of what you just watched, pilots and other premieres are featured.

Gambling

> The Super Bowl has been an integral part of America's sporting fabric and a highlight of the betting year since long before the Supreme Court's ruling last year made it legal in more jurisdictions…$159M bet legally in Nevada…as high as $4.6B illegally.
>
> —Joe Drape, "Sports Betting: An Emerging National Pastime." (2019, B10)

Accounting for the year's biggest wagers, our obsession with gambling and the Super Bowl have been natural partners almost from the start. While it took a few games before the media, the viewers, and Las Vegas realized its "potential," TheSportsGeek.com now declares the Super Bowl to be "the biggest sports betting event of them all and the world's premier entertainment showcase." More money in the United States, we learn, is spent on Super Bowl betting than on any other event, and the NFL is projected to earn $270M in revenue this year from sports betting and gambling deals. In terms of actual games, here are the key sportsbooks winners:

For Super Bowl LV/2021, the legal amount bet was $136M at Nevada sportsbooks, betfirm.com (Jones 2021) reminding us that the Nevada State Gaming

Game	Outcome	Profit
Super Bowl L11/2018	Philadelphia Eagles 41-33 New England Patriots	$158.6M
Super Bowl L111/2019	New England Patriots 13-3 Los Angeles Rams	$145.9M
Super Bowl L1/2017	New England Patriots 34-28 Atlanta Falcons	$138.5M
Super Bowl 50/2016	Denver Broncos 24-10 Carolina Panthers	$132.5M
Super Bowl XL1X/2015	New England Patriots 28-24 Seattle Seahawks	$115.9M

Control Board releases their numbers from 190 sportsbooks. Those sportsbooks are of course part of the drill whereby the house always wins, with a few aberrant exceptions that keep bookies coming back for more. Beyond that, the American Gaming Association estimates that some 97 percent of bets, 23.2M Americans—estimated at $4.5B, are technically illegal.

CNBC reported how, even despite COVID-19 and a 37 percent decline from the previous year, half of all American bet on the big game for 2021. To give you a sense of that, according to sportsbetteringdime.com (McEwan 2021), these are the biggest bets placed for Super Bowl LV/2021, most bettors wagering at least $100:

Bet	Type of Bet	Amount Wagered	Potential Profit
Buccaneers +3.5 (−127)	Spread	$3,460,000	$2,724,409
Buccaneers +3.5 (−115)	Spread	$2,300,000	$2,000,000
Buccaneers to Win (+135)	Moneyline	$1,000,000	$1,350,000
Chiefs–3 (−120)	Spread	$520,000	$433,333
Buccaneers +3.5 (−115)	Spread	$345,000	$300,000
Chiefs to Win (−150)	Moneyline	$300,000	$200,000
Under 56.5 (−110)	Total	$205,000	$186,363
Chiefs to Win (−180)	Moneyline	$180,000	$100,000
Chiefs −3 (−120)	Spread	$120,000	$100,000
Chiefs −3.5 (−115)	Spread	$115,000	$100,000

Bet	Type of Bet	Amount Wagered	Potential Profit
Chiefs –3.5 (–110)	Spread	$110,000	$100,000
Chiefs to Win (–165)	Moneyline	$100,000	$60,606

With fewer people using a sportsbook, bookie, or office pool for betting, Super Bowl 2021 reportedly found more gambling online and between family and friends. Still, according to LendingTree, Americans alone bet $4.3B (down some $2.5B from 2020). The legality of gambling is on a state-by-state basis—available at legalsuperbowlbetting.com, which reads:

> Sports betting is the one form of gambling entertainment in the United States in which the Federal Government has enacted laws to prevent. Until 2018, the Professional and Amateur Sports Protection Act of 1992 (PASPA) law prevented 46 US-states from enacting sports betting legislation until the Supreme Court decided that the ban was unconstitutional. The only states that were exempted from PASPA were Nevada, Oregon, Montana, and Delaware.

So, if you hold a friendly bet about which team will win, what was the best ad, who was the best sportscaster, who will be voted Move Valuable Player (MVP), and the like, take out your calculator. Then there are bets about how long the national anthem might take (over or under one minute, forty-three seconds?), whether there will be overtime, what the ratings will be, whether sportscasters will bring up current events, how the stock market will react the next day, how often various people or players or even their families will be highlighted, whether football-specific issues such as point conversions or coach's challenges will occur, and other betting points that I bet only you could imagine.

Sports analyst Frank Deford (2009) points out that one of the best points about Super Sunday is that "It has done such a wonderful job of appropriating those more discriminating citizens who do not worship Saint Pigskin." Non-fans' money is just as valuable as rabid followers, and whether they are at the party for the food, the pre-game and/or half-time shows, or simply to partake in the revelry, there is something for everyone. "Unlike most official holidays," Deford (2009) reminds us, "Super Bowl Sunday is a whole season, like Christmas. The fourteen days of Super Bowl begin after the conference championships. On the tenth day of Super Bowl my true love gave to me ten scalpers scalping, three photo ops, two quarterbacks, and a point spread from a bookie."

The betting genre is alive and well, including the following: Francis Brown, *Handicapping the NFL: Win Consistently Year after Year* (2013); Gregory Capello, *The Guide to NFL Investing: The Football Betting System of an Investment Professional* (2012); Robert L. Carneiro, *Diary of a Football Handicapper* (2006); Daniel Fabrizio and Jim Cee, *Sports Investing: NFL Betting Systems* (2010); Dan Gordon, *Beat the Sports Book: An Insider's Guide to Betting the NFL*, 2nd ed. (2008); William Hall, *Get in and Win Pro Football Playbook: For Predicting Scores and Placing Winner Wagers by a Wall Street Investment Manager*, 2nd ed. (2013); Michael Konik, *The Smart Money: How the World's Best Sports Bettors Beat the Bookies Out of Millions* (2008); Augie Manfredo, *How I Make Money Betting NFL Football* (2012); David McIntire, *Swimming with the Sharps: A Football Season Spent in Las Vegas* (2013); Tobias Moskowitz and L. Jon Wertheim, *Scorecasting: The Hidden Influences Behind How Sports Are Played and Games Are Won* (2012); Bobby Smith, *How to Beat the Pro Football Points Spread: A Comprehensive, No-Nonsense Guide to Picking NFL Winners* (2008).

It is known that the Monday following Super Bowl calls to Gamblers Anonymous increase substantially. Worse, it is also known that lost productivity that day exceeds $3B, Lexology.com reporting that it begins early in the week whereby US employers lose $820M+ before the game even begins. Superstitions abound. Allen St. John (2010) cites the standard myth that, when an old AFL team wins the game, the stock market will decline during the calendar year and, if an original NFL team wins, the Dow Jones industrial average will rise. The ninth edition of Mario F. Triola's *Elementary Statistics* included this omen:

Stocks Skid on Superstition of Patriot Win

The above *New York Post* headline is a statement about the *Super Bowl Omen*, which states that a Super Bowl victory by a team with NFL origins is followed by a year in which the New York Stock Exchange index rises; otherwise, it falls. (In 1970, the NFL and AFL merged into the current NFL.) This indicator has been correct in 29 of the past 35 years, largely due to the fact that NFL teams win more often, and the stock market tends to rise over time. Forecasting and predicting are important goals of statistics and investment advisors, but common sense suggests that no one base investments on the outcome of one football game. Other indicators used to forecast stock market performance include rising skirt hemlines, aspirin sales, limousines on Wall Street, orders for cardboard boxes, sales of beer versus wine, and elevator traffic at the New York Stock Exchange.

The Role of Media: Ratings, Sportscasters, and Social Media

> The Super Bowl's rise to the zenith of national pop culture events is no accident, but rather due to a savvy marketing strategy that has been amped up over recent years. Through a combination of better cooperation with its television partners, marketing to women and a not-so-subtle linking of football to patriotism, the NFL has managed to expand its reach while most other television properties have shrunk.
>
> —Joe Flint, "How the NFL Turned the Super Bowl into a Phenomenon." (2011)

Michael R. Real (1975), the first Communications scholar to write how the Super Bowl was a "mythic spectacle," suggested how it drew on symbolic forms of personal identification, heroic archetypes, communal focus, spatial and temporal frames of reference, and ecologically regulatory mechanisms. Reflecting on these attributes of mythic function in terms of telesport during the Super Bowl's Fiftieth anniversary, Real and Wenner (2017, 211–212) call the super spectacles an "end game…a result of its unique mythic functioning and structures coming together to shape sensibilities. In that game, we suggest that three overarching and interlocking forces—technology, history, and nation—continue to play an outsized role." Myth and spectacle contemplate if and/or how the game and television are mutually interdependent—a kind of "Who 'invented' whom, Howard Cosell or Muhammed Ali?" If television is credited with popularizing the Super Bowl back in the 1960s, today television owes a debt to the NFL for this communal day when such large audiences tune into a single channel. *Fortune* (Colvin 2021) points out how, "Of last year's 20 most-watched TV broadcasts, 14 were NFL games. The league provided 33 of the top 50 programs and 71 of the top 100, according to Nielsen viewership data."

In the beginning, fans were fortunate to be able to listen to the Super Bowl on transistor radios or watch them on black-and-white television sets—if usually in sports bars. Once TVs became more reasonable in price, and in color, the game was a natural. Although the United States has produced numerous successful sidelines relative to its favorite sport (e.g., novels, films, even fantasy football), media has always figured into the phenomenon of the Super Bowl.

Think of how far we have come media-wise, along with the continued folk tradition of sports talk radio, when the Super Bowl can be streamed for watching on apps, tablets, interactive websites, and even on cellphones. NFL

Now, a personalized video service that provides the latest news, analyses, and highlights, was introduced in 2014. And, going full circle now that it is digital, football can also be heard on various radio stations and/or via NFL Game Pass.

For its February 2020 issue, *Sports Illustrated* circled back to reimagining the Super Bowl by featuring some legends of the game, the lead article, by Michael Rosenberg, Beginning thus: "Brilliant performances, big gambles and some very bizarre behavior." Part of a bigger plan to include still-living MVPs, that list includes Joe Namath, Chuck Howley, Lynn Swann, Terry Bradshaw, Jerry Rice, Steve Young, John Elway, Peyton Manning and Drew Brees.

Ratings

Those of us who monitor the media have a kind of mantra about how twenty-nine of the thirty most-watched television broadcasts of all time have been Super Bowls, 2015 having the largest reported audience of 114.4M. Let me list at least the Top Ten rankings of the most-viewed television shows:

Rank	Broadcast (and Year)	# of Viewers
1	Super Bowl XL1X/2015	114,442,000
2	Super Bowl XLVIII/2014	112,191,000
3	Super Bowl 50/2016	111,864,000
4	Super Bowl XLVI/2012	111,346,000
5	Super Bowl LI/2017	111,319,000
6	Super Bowl XLV/2011	111,041,000
7	Super Bowl XLVII/2013	108,693,000
8	Super Bowl XLIV/2010	106,476,000
9	M*A*S*H Finale 1983	105,970,000
10	Super Bowl LII/2018	103,471,000

If this list were extended, you could see that Super Bowl has long dominated ratings—that M*A*S*H finale breaking a sequence, but all the next twenty highest-ranked television shows were Super Bowls, #30 on the list being Super Bowl X1X/1985 with a viewership of 85,530,000. There had been concern about what would happen in the time of COVID-19, but Super Bowl L1V/2020 came through at #11 with a viewership of 100,466,000; even for its lowest audience in fifteen years, it still had sold-out commercial time.

In 2018, the Media Education Foundation (MEF) crunched the numbers and found that, in answer to "What are you watching when you watch the Super Bowl?" the answer was that viewers are mostly watching commercials, promos, and appeals. The ball was in play, they found, only 8 percent of the entire broadcast (eighteen minutes, forty-three seconds). Think about that! Sut Jhally, MEF executive director's documentary advertising at the Edge of Apocalypse, reports that

> The ball isn't in play a whole lot, and there's a lot of standing around, so corporations have seized the opportunity to stuff their brands and pitches into all that available time and space. They're constantly trying to sell you stuff during the game, while the commercial breaks themselves keep getting longer and longer. Especially during the Super Bowl.

This view is especially prescient as the NFL recently reversed its long-held distancing from betting to now embracing ads for it. "As betting on football ballooned into a multi-billion-dollar industry," the *New York Times* (Drape and Hsu 2021) outlined, "and, as state after state acted to legalize it, the NFL was left with a stark choice: to continue to fight gambling on its games, or to embrace it in exchange for a significant cut of casino marketing dollars."

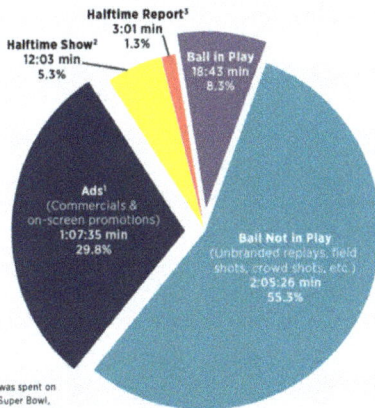

What are you watching when you watch the Super Bowl?

Total Time from Kickoff to End of Super Bowl LI = 3 hours and 46 minutes

Halftime Report[3]
3:01 min
1.3%

Halftime Show[2]
12:03 min
5.3%

Ball in Play
18:43 min
8.3%

Ads[1]
(Commercials &
on-screen promotions)
1:07:35 min
29.8%

Ball Not in Play
(unbranded replays, field
shots, crowd shots, etc.)
2:05:26 min
55.3%

© 2018

1. According to Ad Age, $385 million was spent on in-game advertising during the 2017 Super Bowl, and $419 million is projected to be spent this year.
2. Represents unbranded content during Halftime Show
3. Represents unbranded content during Halftime Report

MEDIA EDUCATION
FOUNDATION
www.mediaed.org

Sportscasters

Curt Gowdy (1919–2006), known by us New Englanders as the beloved "Voice of the (Boston) Red Sox," broadcast the first Super Bowl for NBC in 1967, Ray Scott and Jack Whitaker play-by-play announcers by CBS, Frank Gifford as color commentator, and Pat Summerall (2010) as sideline reporter. Jack "The Almighty" Buck (1924–2002) holds the all-time record of having broadcast the Super Bowl seventeen times, but some others have included Dick Enberg, Greg Gumble (five times), Charlie Jones, Verne Lundquist, John Madden, Jim Nantz, Phil Simms (2005), Bob Trumpy, and no doubt others of your favorites. Betty Cuniberti, the first female in the Dodgers' press box, was also the first woman granted access to an NFL team (the Minnesota Vikings), covering them in the 1970s from training to the Super Bowl; featured in ESPN's 2013 documentary *Let Them Wear Towels*, Cuniberti became the first woman sports reporter at the *San Francisco Chronicle*, later moving to the *Washington Post*. "Half the human race was shut out of this profession for no good reason," she is famous for declaring—especially relative to the locker room issue. In 1992, Leslie Visser became the first—and only woman—to handle the Vince Lombardi trophy presentation, breaking another barrier in 1995 by becoming the first woman to sideline report at Super Bowl XX1X, and she eventually covered twenty-eight Super Bowls. Bonnie Bernstein also made the record books when, for Super Bowl XXXVII/2004, she served as both network radio and television correspondent for the same broadcast (Fuller 2008).

During the pandemic of Super Bowl LV/2021, veteran *New York Times* sports editor Benjamin Hoffman described his twelfth such coverage:

> The entire week felt considerably different. Instead of spending Monday through Friday in hotel conference rooms with players, we were at home talking to them on Zoom. I arrived in Tampa on Friday—typically when a Super Bowl city has reached a fever pitch—and found it to have the feel of much earlier in the week. The various signs of a Super Bowl being in town—the blocked-off streets, the pop-up vendors, the N.F.L. gear being worn everywhere—were there, but the crowds seemed much smaller, and the media gatherings were nonexistent.

Social Media

At first, various social media tried to figure out its role vis-à-vis the Super Bowl, but it didn't take long before it not only became indispensable but actually profitable. If creative commercials were passed on to friends early on, soon roles were reversed and advertisers had users vote, play games, and generally interact with them. In addition to having multi-million-dollar marketing contracts with various advertisers, Facebook, Twitter, and YouTube also share profits on Super Bowl advertising with the NFL. Tweets and memes proliferate and keep it in our thoughts long after the actual game is over. You may recall the GoDaddy racy ad that led viewers to its website for further viewing (it since has rebranded itself from that sexism), TurboTax's challenge, Chipotle's campaign to get users to create their own Free Delivery Sundays ads, Mountain Dew's competition with Pepsi, and many more. Social media, developing as an industry beyond any previous predictions, has been invaluable to the phenomenon of Super Bowl interactions. If you don't believe it, just check out #SuperBowl—more than half of the ads include them.

When the NFL and the players union formed a new ten-year labor agreement on March 15, 2020, part of the ratifications included a 1-percentage-point increase in league revenue sharing for the players, but the bigger news was relaxation on restrictions on marijuana usage such that testing would take place only during the first two weeks of training camp and that those who tested positively would no longer be suspended. Slow to join MLB and the NBA in loosening these restrictions, NFL players apparently "pushed for a relaxed marijuana policy in part because of mounting research that details the hazards of alternatives—including the addiction rates among prescription opioid users and the irreversible internal damage that can be caused by opioid and nonsteroidal anti-inflammatory drugs" (Belson 2020, D1).

## CHAPTER 4

Sociocultural Aspects of the Super Bowl

Though Superman, superhighways, supermarkets, supersonic transport, and other superlatives existed prior to the first Super Bowl in 1966, the cultural work of the Super Bowl is an influential precursor to the era of super sizing.

—Michael Mooradian Lupro, "The Super in the Super Bowl." (2013, 93)

It becomes increasingly clear that football in general and the Super Bowl particularly continue to evolve as a sociocultural force relative to demographics such as racism, gender, ethnicity, and even religion and rhetoric. The NFL launched a campaign called "Inspire Change" in 2019 toward social justice, described by Rugg (2019) as "at once a strategic expansion by the league that seeks to capitalize on the emergent activist power of professional players to build the league's brand as an authoritative and inclusive American institution contributing to social good." As has been argued throughout this book, analyzing the language behind these topics is critical to understanding Super Bowl in the midst of protests and a pandemic.

Fandom for the Super Bowl

If there is one thing I have learned while researching the nature of sports fandom, it is to never say never, because what we enjoy so much about athletic contests are the inherent unpredictability…Sports are the last great unknown.

—Larry Olmsted, "The Lessons We Can Learn from Sports Fandom." (2021)

There is a joke that goes around various sports to the effect that a man at the Super Bowl finds an empty seat and asks the person next to it if it is free. "Yes, it was my wife's, but she's passed away" is the reply. "So sorry," the man responds, but then asks why he didn't invite anyone else to take the seat. The answer: "Everyone's at the funeral." Humor typically has a truth to it, as Super Bowl fans well know. What they don't know, however, is what will happen, which is why football—unscripted and dramatic—is so addictive, occurring as it does in real time.

It is a known fact that the NFL encourages boisterous support—the "BE LOUD AND BE PROUD," "Let's Go Crazy," "Pump it Up," 90-decibel kind of fan noise that Hagood and Vogan (2016) say demonstrates how the league has gone from regulating to cultivating it. While positive in terms of sociability, Super Bowl fandom ranges from pleasurable to addictive. Fans report being born into their allegiances—having it in their blood, so to speak, for what is clearly a bloodsport. Osborne and Coombs (2016, 117) cite the example of Donna who, although a move has surrounded her with Ravens fans, still sees her identity as being defined as a Saints fan:

> There's nothing like being a Saints fan. Nothing will take me being a Saints fan away from me…I will root for the Saints until whenever, even if they're going up against a team I want to do to the Super Bowl, I will root for the Saints—I *have* to root for the Saints.

Many fans, both male and female, participate in competition called Fantasy Football, playing virtual general managers who make up imaginary teams whose players might earn them money depending on their actual football playing. Started in California in 1962, the inaugural league was the Greater Oakland Professional Pigskin Prognosticators League (GOPPPL), their rosters including the following: two quarterbacks, four halfbacks, two fullbacks, four wide receivers/tight ends, two kick/punt returners, two kickers, two defensive backs/linebackers, and two defensive linemen. Scoring is based on real-life games, points given to specific plays such as a touchdown pass, a field goal, kickoff, or punt. In 2017, the Fantasy Sports & Gaming Association (FSGA) reported 59.3M players—many playing with the Draft Kings or FanDuel, the industry valued at $7.2B. During the COVID-19 pandemic, a number of clever teams had names such as Quaranteam, Kamravirus, Drew Lockdown, Never Leaving Mahomes, SaQuarantine Barkley, Keep Calm and Kerryone, Jalen Hurd Immunity, and the like. To give you a sense of how the game works, these were the Top 5 fantasy running back rankings for the Fifty-Fifth Super Bowl:

- Leonard Fournette, Tampa Bay Buccaneers
- Darrel Williams, Kansas City Chiefs
- Ronald Jones II, Tampa Bay Buccaneers
- Clyde Edwards-Helaire, Kansas City Chiefs
- Le'Veon Bell, Kansas City Chiefs

Fandom for the Super Bowl, it must be noted, is certainly not limited to American audiences, even if we know that the American Forces Network (AFN) sends the game to military members in foreign outposts. With reports of global audiences of more than a billion, it makes sense that our Canadian and Mexican neighbors might be interested, but we also find that Super Bowls are beamed to Europe, Asia, Australia, and some two hundred other countries. Particularly at home, it has long been noted that advertisers "tend to assume that American football fans are straight men" (Esmonde 2017), so sexy/sexist commercials have prevailed.

When Michael Jackson performed at Super Bowl XXVII/1993 during halftime, it raised the ratings sky-high to 133.4M viewers—a million-dollar performance that remains one of the most-watched events in American media history. Sandomir (2009) declared that his legacy would forever include the title King of Pigskin:

> Jackson produced a stunning first: raising NBC's halftime rating higher than the Super Bowl action before it. The NFL had grasped the need to enlist big-name, contemporary, broad-appeal artists to keep viewers from straying. So, it used Jackson to continue expanding the notion of the Super Bowl as a mega-event that includes a game.

As the NFL does not pay for half-time appearances, it and Frito-Lay instead decided to donate $100,000 to Jackson's Heal the World Foundation and allocated commercial airtime for an appeal to its "Heal L.A." campaign to provide drug education, healthcare, and mentorship to young people in the aftermath of riots there. When the King of Pop appeared on the *Oprah Winfrey Show*, February 10, 1993, "Michael Jackson talks to Oprah" drew the largest television ratings in history for an interview—$62.30M (by comparison, her March 12, 2021 her explosive interview with Meghan Markle and Prince Harry attracted 17.1M viewers).

Mike Powell (Source: Getty Images)

Gender Issues

With NFL Commissioner Roger Goodell claiming that 47 percent of its fan base is made up of women (Graham and Young 2020), the organization nevertheless continues to belittle their abilities—using them in rigid roles as cheerleaders, dancers, and performers, and basically as promotional sex objects, if occasionally recognizing the rare female sports announcer. The central action, as Michael R. Real (1989, 198) points out, is a "masculine preserve." Underscored by militaristic roots and rhetoric, Gerald R. Gems (2019, xi) points out how, in the early days of football, "Only males were allowed to be school cheerleaders because it was assumed no male spectators would follow the directions of a female." As recently as 2021, a group of female workers accused the NFL of what they described as a stifling, demoralizing corporate culture, far from a safe place when incidents are all excused in the name of football.

Cheerleaders/Cheerleading

> Cheerleading occupies a contested space in American culture and a key point of controversy is whether it ought to be considered a sport…The gender politics at work here illustrate both the elasticity of gender categories and the limits of that elasticity, as gendered boundaries are drawn and redrawn between what gets to count as sport and what does not, and as cheerleading simultaneously challenges and reinforces the notion of sport as a male preserve.
>
> —Grindstaff and West. "Cheerleading and the Gendered Politics of Sport."
> *Social Problems* (2006)

Oh, how cheerleading and cheerleaders have changed. Although early football's cheerers were men, CNN (McGown 2013) now questions whether the NFL's cheerleaders are gratuitous sexism or all-American fun: "Entertainment or titillation? Bright eyes, sparkling white teeth, big hair and barely covered breasts, these are the women whose gyrating hips bring a hint of glamour to National Football League fields from New England to California." The Baltimore Colts became, in 1954, the first NFL team to have cheerleaders, but it was the scantily clad Dallas Cowboys Cheerleaders (DCC)—officially nicknamed "America's Sweethearts," who set the standard for complex dance routines, and they became so accomplished they established their own reality television show in 2006 called *Dallas Cowboys Cheerleaders: Making the Team*. Mary Ellen

Hanson (1995, 52) argues that they set the standard for future NFL cheerleading ("go-go dancers on the sidelines") teams. And then there were the Honey Bears, "dancing girls" hired by Chicago Bears owner George "Papa Bear" Halas in 1976 as a scheme to boost team morale. They were instant and constant hits for nearly a decade, and it has been noted that the Bears have not won a Super Bowl since they were disbanded ten years later after one of them posed nude for *Playboy*; since then, the "Curse of the Honey Bears" has lingered.

The Buffalo Bills, worth $935M, have also been questioned as to why their cheerleaders earn so little—($150/game day). Although adhering to grueling practice and game-day schedules—30 to 40+ hours/week, fined for forgetting their pom-poms or gaining weight, their wages are far below minimum standards. On the opposite side of the issue, however, just recently some NFL cheerleaders have sued their teams in litigation over wage discrimination and hostile work environments, a key example being the Washington Redskins cheerleaders expected to pose topless for beachside photos. Only six of the thirty-two NFL teams do not have cheerleaders—Chicago Bears, Buffalo Bills, Cleveland Browns, NY Giants, Green Bay Packers, and Pittsburgh Steelers, and what do they have in common? Open-air stadiums, which really are tough to be in, never mind in skimpy outfits. Super Bowl L111/2019 had male cheerleaders for the first time ever, Quinton Peron and Napoleon Jinnies joining the squad for the Los Angeles Rams and opening the door for others. Super Bowl LV/2021 was the first one without cheerleaders of either gender in forty-five years, Pittsburgh Steelers getting rid of them in 1970 by what was billed as an "organizational decision" and Green Bay Packers having done away with them in 1988 after their market research found fans didn't care much about cheerleaders. Third-wave feminism also played a role, the women wanting to be taken more seriously for their sport than for their looks. "For decades, female athletes were relegated to the sidelines—physically and metaphorically speaking," Hindman and Walker (2021) have noted.

> Cheerleaders have challenged the negative stereotypes by making cheerleading a sport on their own terms. Through personal agency, these girls embrace a powerful image of the cheerleader—one that fuses identities of femininity and athleticism. For these girls, it is not a choice between being a cheerleader or jock, girlie or athletic. Instead, they create a blended identity by keeping the feminine markers of a cheerleader while focusing on a competitive role rather than a supportive one.

Females and Football

Whether you need a tutorial or want to know what resources are out there directed at women "needing" to know more about football, here is a list of belittling books:

1. Caron, Sandra L., and J. Michael Hodgson. 2011. *Tackling Football: A Woman's Guide to Understanding the Game.* "Women are not only fans, but also players, cheerleaders, trainers, reporters, sports information directors, and coaches, and on occasion, officials, commentators and athletic directors."

2. Gagnier, Suzanna. 2007. *Putting on the Blitz: The Football Book for Women.* "Don't get left out this season. Football is more fun than (sic) you can imagine…This book is awesome on the coffee table…Trust me, she will love it."

3. Green, Sarah A. 2011. *Football, the Basics for Women.*

> Have you always wanted to know the difference between a kickoff and a punt kick? Ever been embarrassed to ask what the referee is doing with his arms? Have you heard of Fantasy Football, but have no idea what it is? The old cliché about the way to a man's heart…I believe that sports can be another way to your guy's heart…You still want to be part of the enjoyment he experiences when he watches it. Girl, this book is written for you.

4. Malamuet, Melissa. 2010. *She's Got Game: The Woman's Guide to Loving Sports (or Just How to Fake It!)* "Sporting events raise so many questions… What do I *wear*? Will I wipe out if I wear heels? Should I wear makeup? And how *do* you say that player's name?…The ultimate guide to enjoying yourself (and looking smart) at any sporting event."

5. Newell, A. J. 2012. *Gaga for Gridiron: The Ultimate Guide to Football for Women.* The way to a man's heart may be through his stomach, but the way to his brain is through football. If you are like most women, you know by now that men speak "footballese."

6. Nicholas, Alice. 2007. *Talk Football: Written by a Woman for Women Who Want to Speak America's Gridiron Language.* "The GO TO football book for beginners."

7. Peete, Holly Robinson, and Daniel Paisner. 2005. *Get Your Own Damn Beer, I'm Watching the Game!: A Woman's Guide to Loving Pro Football.* "Year after year, Sunday afternoons and Monday nights during the NFL season have belonged to men. While they cheer and argue play calls, the women in their lives are relegated to beer and chip detail. It's time for these women to join the action."

8. Saucedo-Artino, Teresa. 2000. *Football for Females: The Women's Survival Guide to the Football Season.* "Are you tired of being a football widow? Would you like to join in the fun but are embarrassed by your lack of knowledge of the sport of football—even though you know you're smarter than the men who sit in your living room every Sunday?"

But there is encouragement, Ashley M. Rockwell (2016) pointing out "a general trajectory toward more gender-egalitarian messaging" in Super Bowl ads. From a content analysis of 665 commercials from 2005 to 2016, she found narratives shifting toward an emphasis on "fatherhood, caring men, and tough women." And in this discussion about gender, it should also be added that the Super Bowl, while oftentimes considered a "testosterone-driven male event," at the same time offers a Prime Time for male bonding. Cooper and Tang (2018) did find that women tend to engage in non-football elements during the actual playing of the Super Bowl, while men indicated being more interested in the game itself.

More good news was witnessed at Super Bowl LV/2021, Alex Azzi (2021) pointing out women who have written their way in history books: referee Sarah Thomas as the first woman to officiate a Super Bowl and Tampa Bay Buccaneers assistant coaches Maral Javadifar and Lori Locust, the first female coaches to win a Super Bowl. The editor of *On Her Turf* for NBCSports reviews earlier successes:

- On December 27, 1987, Gayle Sierens became the first woman to ever call play-by-play of an NFL game when she was in the booth for NBC's broadcast of the Seattle Seahawks-Kansas City Chiefs. However, thirty years would pass until a second woman—Beth Mowins—followed in Sieren's footsteps.
- In 1997, Amy Trask (2016) became the chief executive of the Oakland Raiders, the first woman to hold that role in the NFL, went on to work for the Raiders for nearly thirty years.

- In 2020, Katie Sowers—an assistant coach for the San Francisco 49ers—became the first woman to coach in the Super Bowl. Sowers, who was also the first openly gay coach in the NFL, discussed her career in *Football Is Female*.
- January 2021, Jennifer King was promoted to assistant running backs coach of the Washington Football Team, making her the first Black woman to serve as a full-time NFL coach.

Add to that litany the fact that, in 1975, Jeannie Morris became the first woman to report live from the Super Bowl and that Jen Welter (2017) became the first female coach in NFL history when, in 2015, the Arizona Cardinals hired her to an intern position. And more, Kathryn Smith became the NFL's first full-time female coach when she was named special teams' quality control coach for the Buffalo Bills in 2016.

It might surprise you to know that women hold primary ownership stakes in several NFL teams: Bears (Virginia Halas McCaskey), Bills (Kim Pegula), Browns (Dee Haslam), 49ers (Denise DeBartolo York), Lions (Martha Firestone Ford), Raiders (Carol Davis), Saints (Gayle Benson), and Titans (Amy Adams Strunk). Georgian Frontiere oversaw the Los Angeles vs. St. Louis Rams in three Super Bowls (X1V, XXX1V, and XXXVI) under her majority ownership winning the 1999 one which later earned the moniker, the "Dot-com Super Bowl," because of the number of internet-related advertisers.

Before leaving the topic of gender, let me also introduce the topic of LGBTIQ, since the Super Bowl has incorporated commercials relative to gayness for at least a decade but only recently has become relaxed about the topic. Every time a football player comes out—following in the footsteps of Michael Sam of the St. Louis Rams in 2014, the first publicly gay player drafted by the NFL—it becomes news, and yet it was really something when Cowboys linebacker Jeff Rohrer had a same-sex marriage in 2018.

Sex Trafficking and the Super Bowl

Wherever the Super Bowl is being held, there has been shown to be a 300% increase in online sex trafficking.

—Francine Rivers. 2016. "The Dark Side of the Super Bowl." February 2, 2016. http://francinerivers.com/the-dark-side-of-the-super-bowl/

Depending on your source, the topic of sex trafficking and the Super Bowl could be considered a controversial issue (e.g., Martin and Hill 2019; Reason. com); however, when Richard Lapchick, Director of the University of Central Florida's Institute for Diversity and Ethics in Sport, addresses the topic, it is worth a review. In a 2020 report, Lapchick begins by pointing out how, according to the UN-backed International Labor Organization (ILO), some 40M people are affected by this industry that reportedly earns $150B/year. Florida, it turns out, ranks third nationwide in this activity, Ziba Cranmer (2011) reporting how experts declared that "as many as 10,000 prostitutes descended on last year's Super Bowl in Miami, many of whom were trafficked." When Super Bowl L1V/2020 returned, the city's hotel industry hosted an anti-trafficking summit to alert and train staff to recognize its signs. Ahead of Super Bowl LV/2021, *Newsweek* (Dutton 2021) revealed that undercover detectives in Tampa arrested seventy people in a prostitution sting called Operation Interception, the sheriff reporting, "All of these men have one thing in common: they did not care if the women they were going to have sex with were being exploited, forced to sell their bodies against their will." Those arrested included active military members, a banker, a Christian schoolteacher, construction workers, and two registered sex offenders.

Dominique Roe-Sepowitz, James Gallagher, and Kristine Hickle of The McCain Institute at the University of Arizona (mccaininstitute.org) produced a 2014 exploration on the topic, "most of which indicates it is a key variable leading to a dramatic increase in commercial sexual exploitation and victimization…with estimates of as many as 10,000 victims flooding host cities." Much of the activity is hidden, according to Roe-Sepowitz, director of the Office of Sex Trafficking Intervention Research at Arizona State University, who has determined that "The victims, buyers and sellers are all doing this behind a curtain, so it's difficult to capture what's happening." For Super Bowl XL1X/2015 in Phoenix, she and fellow researchers found an uptick in online sex ads, pimps admitting they were important marketing tools. While some call this a myth, sting operations like Operation Guardian Angel after Super Bowl L1/2017 yielded ninety-four human trafficking results (mostly Asian women) and the games in general continue to be considered "a bonanza for traffickers." We certainly don't want to focus on this seedy side of the Super Bowl, but we need to raise awareness of the issue. Consider this comment from the *It's a Penalty Campaign*: "When someone traffics drugs, they can only sell those drugs one time. But when you traffic human beings, you can sell them over and over and make a lot of money." In 2015, the US House of Representatives pushed for a bipartisan crackdown on human trafficking, which human rights activists have likened to slavery, proposed legislation including safe-harbor laws for victims and strong penalties for traffickers.

Jennifer E. Fredericks (2016) content-analyzed escort ads during Super Bowl 50 and found a strong link between major sporting events and sex trafficking; citing literature and research about profits made by transporting victims to cities for commercial sex during sporting events, they declared the Super Bowl to be the biggest, although exact numbers remain unknown due to the underground nature of the trafficking. One of the best-known such escorts is actress Emily Ratajkowski, who wore a tiny black leather tube dress for the 13th annual "Leather & Laces" mega party at Super Bowl 50/2016. According to the Rojak Daily Team of gempak.com, her modeling agent arranged a date with Malaysian businessman Low Taek Jho (aka Jho Low), who reportedly paid her RM103,000 ($25,000) to be his date. In her autobiographical tell-all *My Body* (Metropolitan Books 2021), Ratajkowski describes the event claiming that she had no idea what was expected of her during the outing but simply accepted the assignment. These and other seedy stories like those in the 2012 Super Bowl–inspired documentary *Tricked* are all part of the dark side of the games. Laura Dimon (2014) talks about that dark side that television viewers might not know about; reporting on Super Bowl XLVIII/2014 that was to be played at MetLife Stadium in East Rutherford, NJ, she wrote:

> Before fans cheer, shout, and drink plenty of beer celebrating the ultimate all-American tradition, they will place their hands on their hearts for Renee Fleming's national anthem, and sing praise to the United States of America... (unaware) that America's most popular sporting event has also been called out as one of the largest venues for human trafficking in the world.

She reports how, according to the New Jersey Coalition against Human Trafficking, along with tens of thousands of fans, "it also attracts a sector of violence, organized criminal activity that operates in plain sight without notice including human trafficking in both the sex and labor industries."

In anticipation of Super Bowl XLIX/2015, *National Catholic Register* (Hadro 2015) reported how the US House of Representatives was pushing for a bipartisan crackdown on sex trafficking—considered "modern-day slavery" by human rights advocates. Representative Chris Smith (R, NJ) introduced the Trafficking Victims Protection Act, hoping it would pass before the game in Glendale, AZ, stating: "Hopefully, the Super Bowl will not see what we've seen in previous Super Bowls, and that is the massive exploitation of women." Kristi Noem (R, SD) signed on, adding that, "Everybody thinks human trafficking and sex trafficking is happening at the Super Bowl, at big events. Well, it's also happening at little, rural, small towns every single day." Acknowledging the roles of Craigslist and the internet (where some 76% of human and sex trafficking takes place), these public servants are critical to recognizing the issue.

Alas, the good news relative to gender and the Super Bowl is that women have come a long way—going from just being showcased as sex objects to been seen instead as symbols of strength. The year 2015 was pivotal, when Jen Welter was hired as a linebackers coach by the Arizona Cardinals and Sarah Thomas became a full-time NFL referee. The next year, Katie Sowers became the first woman to be an assistant coach in a Super Bowl (for the San Francisco 49ers) and Callie Brownson moved from being an intern with the Buffalo Bills to chief of staff of the Cleveland Browns. Advertisers are beginning to take note. Consider: for Super Bowl LIV/2020, Katie Sowers starred in an advertisement for Microsoft Surface, World Cup soccer stars Carli Lloyd and Chrystal Dunn were in a Secret commercial, and Olay had an all-female team of astronauts. "Yet as women in the NFL hope for the days when they are no longer groundbreakers, they appreciate the progress that this weekend represents," noted Brassil and Draper (2021) about the most recent game. After all, don't forget that women make up half the fan base and are known to drive 80 percent of consumer decisions.

Masculinity

> The Super Bowl is a contemporary media spectacle whose hegemonic undertones of misogyny and homophobia communicate to its audience punitive standards of masculinity, gender roles, and the American nation state…The warlike narrative structure of American football reaffirms male superiority over women, teaching men and boys conformity to patriarchal and sexist cultural values.
>
> —Jan Huebenthal. "Quick! Do Something Manly!" (2013, i)

As the Super Bowl is about men, and for men, narratives of hyper-masculinity clearly need to be factored into this discussion, and commercials offer ideal ways to analyze their representations. In 2005, Messner and Montez deOca studied both Super Bowl beer commercials and Sports illustrated print ads from

2002 to 2003, finding "the then newfound emergence of the lovable happy loser trope of masculinity in advertising, which depicted scrawny, nerdy men who fail to get the girl but who can still have a good laugh and a cold brew with their buds," paraphrased by Green and Van Oort (2013, 696), whose study found the following about Super Bowl XL1V/2010 commercials:

> Viewers were bombarded with images of feminized, again, and ultimately powerless male bodies, images that both implicitly and explicitly signaled a much broader crisis wherein the constitutive ingredients of hegemony masculinity has supposedly been lost, stolen, or otherwise altered. (695)

Super Bowl ads continue to reflect and deflect notions of masculinity—think Gillette's toxic masculinity one, and other cases where our rugged heroes are opening up to talking about their feelings (Doan 2019; Krattenmaker 2019; Wenner 2019). Much has been made, too, of men and meat—especially red meat, which Jeffrey Sobal (2006) has labeled "archetypical masculine food." What does it mean—men tend to be carnivores and so they love their steaks?

Finding a general trajectory toward gender-egalitarian messaging from analyzing ads from 2005 to 2016, Ashley M. Rockwell (2016) determined that, "As the economy recovered, advertisers emphasized fatherhood, caring men, and tough women." Clearly, as social consciousness is raised, bullying and sexism lose their heft, and it is especially encouraging that, for a sport based on machismo, the topic of mental health is being brought to the fore.

Racial Issues

> Forget lost puppies and horses, adult-like babies, and weird stunts involving snack foods. Instead, this year's Super Bowl ads will prominently feature social and racial justice issues, along with Covid-19 messages, according to a sports business trade report.
>
> —Bruce Haring, "Super Bowl LV May Double Down on Social and Racial Justice Ads." (2020)

Reflecting on his seven years as an outside linebacker with the St. Louis Cardinals, Dave Meggyesy's 1970 memoir *Out of Their League* stunned readers with his reflections on football as exemplifying the worst of American culture: "There was the incredible racism which I was to see close up in the Cardinals' organization and throughout the league" (146) he wrote, adding, "There was also violence and sadism, not so much on the part of the players or in the game itself, but very much in the minds of the beholders—the millions of Americans who watch football every weekend in something of approaching a sexual frenzy." While less has been written about the histories of football at Historically Black College and University (HBCU) institutions, they matched others in emphasizing masculinity, athletics used as a means to showcase prowess. On another plane, O'Donnell and Spires (2008) point out that "The current dominant official discourse of race in relation to sport in the Western World is that there is no discourse of race: race is emphatically a non-issue"—bringing up a very important point relative to the Super Bowl, especially when nearly three-quarters of the players are Black. While on the one hand it has come a long way from its early days of openly rampant segregation, run the numbers and it is blatantly clear that African American coaches, trainers, and managers are sorely lacking, never mind having roles as owners. White corporations and polarization prevail. Add some advertisements, and it is clear that the NFL has been color-blind to issues of systemic racism—to the point where celebrities like Mariah Carey, Cedric the Entertainer, Serena Williams, Rihanna, Amy Schumer, and others have gone public about it.

While he and Bobby Marshall (1880–1958) were the first African American players in the NFL, Fritz Pollard (1894–1986), playing for the Akron Pros in the 1920, became the first Black named to Walter Camp's All-America team and, eventually, a head coach who founded his own pro football team: the Brown Bombers. Jump to 2007 and Super Bowl XL1 could brag about having two Black head coaches—Tony Dungy of the Indianapolis Colts and Lovie Smith of the Chicago Bears. While the NFL continues to claim it espouses racial diversity and racial unity—especially when some 70 percent of the NFL players are African American, both Blacks and Native Americans would argue that it still has a long way to go.

The Rooney Rule, established in 2003 and named after Dan Rooney, former owner of the Pittsburgh Steelers, is an affirmative action requiring teams to interview ethnic minorities for key coaching and operation jobs; in addition to encouraging the hiring of minority candidates, the policy has been adopted by other companies. Still, of the current thirty-two NFL teams, only four head coaches and two general managers are men of color and only two owners are not white (Pakistani American Shahid Khan of the Jacksonville Jaguars, and Korean American Kim Pegula of the Buffalo Bills—the latter, the only woman. In 2017, the Players Coalition was founded by Anquan Boldin (NFL 2015

Walter Payton Man of the Year) and Malcolm Jenkins (2017 NFLPA Byron "Whizzer" White winner) as a 501(c)(3) "to improve social justice and racial equality in our country." *Atlantic* (Giorgis 2020) discusses a social justice ad that aired during Super Bowl L1V/2020 featuring Boldin talking about his cousin who was killed by a police officer and, yet, somehow never mentioning Colin Kaepernick's "taking a knee" to protest police brutality (Perry 2019). There is some irony there in that the NFL has partnered with rapper/entrepreneur Jay-Z to create both a partnership with his entertainment agency Roc Nation and an apparel line for social progress called "Inspire Change," and yet it distanced itself from Kaepernick for so long—too reflective of football's long ignorance of and (in)action to racial inequities. The NFL's "Inspire Change" ad for Super Bowl LV/2021 featured a narrator declaring that "Football is a microcosm of America"—suggesting that it represents multiculturalism but, in truth, it was far from Nike's 2018 decision to feature Kaepernick and his silent protest (Freeman 2020). Public relations rule.

Some have argued that white nationalism is at the base of the NFL's stance— ranging from the lyrics of *The Star-Spangled Banner*, whose third verse celebrates slavery, to being coerced to "respect" the flag. Cultural appropriation is another slant, and, even though the Washington Redskins changed their name, Kansas City Chiefs fans are accused of racism because they wear face paint, do the "tomahawk chop" salute, and remain oddly respectful about Native American symbols.

Then there is the issue of White flight from tackle football, *Atlantic* (Semuels 2019) reporting how Black boys in lower-income communities are the main ones flocking to football. Reporting on a survey by University of Michigan sociology Philip Veliz that, out of the 500,000 eighth-, tenth-, and twelfth graders who played, 44 percent were Black and 29 percent white. The takeaway: "This divergence paints a troubling picture of how economic opportunity—or a lack thereof—governs which boys are incentivized to put their body and brain at risk to play."

In 2020, former pro football wide receiver Donte Stallworth wrote an op-ed in *New York Times* titled "The NFL Needs More Than a Song." While recognizing the Black Lives Matter (BLM) protests through song and the NFL pledge of $250M to fight systemic racism are a start, what Stallworth was referring to was the need for more Black coaches and executives.

Mascots

> Super Bowl Sunday is a uniquely American celebration of guts and grit, cash and commercialism. It's our annual ritual and favored sport…But before there was the NFL, there were real 49ers who fought against actual chiefs. It was history's Version 1.0 of a non-gridiron battle where native sons fought Native Americans. This partly forgotten fight remains a shameful part of U.S. history. That long-ago chapter is relevant today, at a time when racism and foreign immigration remain hot-button political issues.
>
> —Markos Kounalakis, "The Ugly History of the Super Bowl Teams' Mascots." (2020)

Whether protesting the imitation of indigenous peoples without their approval or succumbing to corporate pressure to please supporters, the topic of Super Bowl mascots has been a touchy one. In 2020, The Cleveland Indians got rid of Chief Wahoo, the Atlanta Braves decided to reconsider their controversial "tomahawk chop" chant, and people wondered whether the Kansas City Chiefs or the Chicago Blackhawks would retire their names, but the Washington Redskins decided to retire their "Redskins" logo. Mostly centered around racism against Native Americans, dealing with cultural appropriation, my friend C. Richard King, Chair of Humanities, History, and Social Sciences at Columbia College Chicago, has been at the front of the argument, as seen in his books *Team Spirits: The Native American Mascot Controversy* (2001) and *Redskins: Insult and Brand* (2016) and his article "Hail to the Chiefs: Race, gender, and Native American Sports Mascots" (2010). Interestingly, the same year that the name changed from the Washington Redskins to the Washington Home Team the first Black team president (Jason Wright) in NFL history was hired. With the further concurrent hiring of Blacks—Martin Mayhew (as general manager), Ron Rivera (as head coach), and Wright (as president)—Washington made history as the first such team.

According to Wikipedia, these are the current mascots of the NFL:

Team	Mascot(s)	Description
Arizona Cardinals	Big Red	Red cardinal
Atlanta Falcons	Freddie Falcon	Caricature of a falcon
Baltimore Ravens	Poe	Raven named by Edgar Allen Poe

Team	Mascot(s)	Description
	Rise and Conquer	Live ravens at the Maryland Zoo
Buffalo Bills	Billy Buffalo	Actual 8′ buffalo
Carolina Panthers	Sir Purr	Black panther-like figure
Chicago Bears	Staley Da Bear	Bear-like figure named for A. E. Staley
Cincinnati Bengals	Who Dey	Orange Bengal-like figure
Cleveland Browns	Chomps, Swagger, Jr., Brownie the Elf	A dog-like, Chomps is based on the team's Dawg Pound while Swagger Jr. is a live bull mastiff
Dallas Cowboys	Rowdy	Caricature of a cowboy
Denver Broncos	Miles Thunder Thunder 11	Miles is a white, horse-like anthropomorphic figure with an orange jersey, and Thunder 11 is a real Arabian horse
Detroit Lions	Roary	Lion-like figure
Green Bay Packers	–	–
Houston Texans	Toro	Toro is a dark bull-like figure
Indianapolis Colt	Blue	Blue is a horse-like figure
Jacksonville Jaguars	Jaxson de Ville	Jaxson de Ville is jaguar-like
Kansas City Chiefs	K. C. Wolf; Warpaint	Warpaint was the original mascot, replaced in 1989 by K. C. Wolf to honor Wolf-pack fans
Las Vegas Raiders	Raider Rusher	Giant head wearing a spiked Raiders helmet with long, skinny arm and legs
Los Angeles Chargers	Boltman	–
Los Angeles Rams	Rampage	Ram-like figure
Miami Dolphins	Dolphin	Dolphin-like figure
Minnesota Vikings	Viktor	Viking caricature
New England Patriots	Pat Patriot	Caricature of a patriot from the American Revolution

Team	Mascot(s)	Description
New Orleans Saints	Gumbo, Sir Saint	Dog-like figure named after gumbo
New York Giants	–	–
New York Jets	–	–
Philadelphia Eagles	Swoop, Air Swoop	Swoop is eagle-like, while Air Swoop is an air-filled eagle caricature
Pittsburgh Steelers	Steely McBeam	A steelworker
San Francisco 49ers	Sourdough Sam	Caricature of a 49er/prospector
Seattle Seahawks	Blitz and Boom; Taima	Blitz and Boom are large, blue anthropomorphic birds while Taima is a live augur hawk
Tampa Bay Buccaneers	Captain Fear	Pirate caricature
Tennessee Titans	T-rac	Raccoon, Tennessee's state animal
Washington Football Team	–	

The Role of Ritual and Religion

There is a remarkable sense in which the Super Bowl functions as a major religious festival for American culture, for the event signals a convergence of sports, politics and myth. Like festivals in ancient societies, which made no distinctions regarding the religious, political and sporting character of certain events, the Super Bowl succeeds in reuniting these now disparate dimensions of social life.

—Joseph L. Price, "The Super Bowl as Religious Festival." (1982)

The pomp and circumstance of the Super Bowl signals the approach of longer lasting festivity.

—Craig A. Forney, *The Holy Trinity of American Sports* (2007, 29)

Super Bowl as Secular Religion

It may be no coincidence that the Super Bowl is played on the Lord's Day—called Super Sunday, steeped as it is in spirituality, sacrifice, and ritualistic fervor. The faithful have a pilgrimage to gather; blind devotion prevails; many players, coaches, and their families profess religion (Eichelberger 2012); and faith in various football players runs deep. Super Bowl has been called "the highest sabbath in the American religion" (Kriegel 2004); "a major religious festival for American culture" (Price 2001); "our 'high holy day'" (Higgs and Braswell 2004, 99); and "the holiest day of the season" (Bishop 2007). According to a April 2, 2012 tweet on ThyBlackMan.com declaring football as "undisputedly America's national religion," Super Bowl XLVI/2012 attracted 57M viewers, an audience *roughly eight and a half times larger* than the paltry 7M viewers and 1M viewers garnered that day, respectively, by the two most popular Christian televangelists in America—Joel Osteen and Pat Robertson.

Practitioners talk about their faith in certain players—worshipping some, being dedicated to certain teams and praying that they will win, suffering if they do not. Others of the faithful, who make the pilgrimage at least to their televisions but fantasize about going to Mecca someday, reveal how emotional and transformative is the escape offered by their worshipping. If *Merriam Webster* defines religion as "a personal set or institutionalized system of religious attitudes, beliefs, and practices," "scrupulous conformity," "commitment or devotion to religious faith or observation," can you see the parallels? Both pre-and post-game programming, which is why networks fight to host the Super Bowl, are often as guilty as commercials of being insensitive to racial and religious beliefs. A case in point is Fox's pushing of its program *24: Legacy* about a jihadist killer in the United States that was deemed "a one-hour Super Bowl ad for Islamophobia." Or, what were the subtexts for Coke having an Arab walking through the desert with a camel, or Jeep's ad with a headscarf-wearing Muslim woman at the wheel? In a survey by the Public Religion Research Institute, Kaleem (2014) reports,

> Half of American sports fans say they believe God or a supernatural force is at play in the games they watch, according to a new survey. That percentage includes Americans who pray for God to help their team (26%), think their team has been cursed (25%) or more generally believe God is involved in determining who wins on the court or in the field (19%).

"The Super Bowl is merely the sport's high holiday," Jason Anthony (2012) has declared. "The entire season is filled with talk of the spirit. Some of the sport's most electric non-Super Bowl moments have been christened 'the Immaculate Reception,' 'the Holy Roller,' and 'the Music City Miracle.' And even regular season games often don't end without one all-or-nothing 'Hail Mary.'" But the phenomenon is not limited to Christians, and Gellman (2013) reported that Super Bowl Sunday has become recognized as a Jewish holiday as it continues to become so pervasive in American culture.

Amazingly, at Super Bowl LV/2021, Pope Francis made an unexpected appearance, sending a video message in Spanish that played on the stadium's jumbotrons about how sporting events like it are "symbolic of peace" in that they can demonstrate the possibility of building "a world of encounter and of peace." Participation in sports, he said, can teach us to go beyond our own self-interests to learning sacrifice and fidelity to rules. Small wonder that some observers have said that the stadium itself is a sacred place.

In the interest of inclusivity, it was notable that Mohammed Sanu, a wide receiver for the San Francisco 49ers and a Muslim by faith, has gone on record wanting to separate his religion from sport; that the Church of Scientology has been airing Super Bowl ads since 2013; that *Times of Israel* (Berman 2021) identified a number of Jewish stories and subplots at Super Bowl LV; and that Bruce Springsteen's 2021 Jeep commercial drew both praise and criticism from the Christian community.

The Violence Factor and Health

> Football, wherein is nothing but beastly fury, and extreme violence, whereof proceedeth hurt, and consequently rancour and malice do remain with them that be wounded.
>
> —Sir Thomas Elyot, *The Boke Named the Governour* (1531)

In much of the world, where *football* (futból) is the term for what Americans call soccer, a phenomenon known as hooliganism is at play; defined as "barbaric behavior perpetrated by spectators," in its extreme it can involve gang conflicts, riot police, and general disorder. In American football, though, the barbarism tends to ritualistically stay on the field as teams wear helmets as they crash full force into one another, "playing hurt" being a badge of honor. Starting with college sports, scandals abound: corruption, inequities of "compensation," locker room prejudices, illegal solicitations by recruiters, trade-offs and violations, gross commercialism, and other factors relative to the dark side of the game. Probably no case better exemplifies the confluence of violence and football than that of Aaron Hernandez (1989–2017), a New England Patriot tight end who was convicted of murder, committed suicide in his jail cell, and was posthumously diagnosed with chronic traumatic encephalopathy (CTE).

As the NFL continues to encourage ever-larger offensive and defensive linemen, average weights keep going over 300+ pounds, and obesity comes with its own share of problems. Yet absolutely nothing compares to the issue of broken bodies due to concussions (Culverhouse 2011; Fainaru-Wada and Fainaru 2013; Hoge 2018; Omaru 2017; Solotaroff 2011), all too often leading to the brain disease CTE. Although just recently recognized by the NFL—which at first dismissed it or tried to have hushed lawsuits taken care of, once scientists at Boston University found CTE risk doubled after two and half playing years and the average pro career is three and quarter years, an overwhelming number of players donated their brains for future research. As of 2020, the NFL agreed to a pittance of $1B in compensation for retired players with head trauma.

"Football's historical prominence in sport media and folk culture has sustained a hegemonic model of masculinity that prioritizes competitiveness, asceticism, success (winning), aggression, violence, superiority to women, and respect for and compliance with male authority," Sabo and Panepinto (1990, 115) have written. Whether framed as a mirror of society, a result of fan behavior, economic incentives, innate aggression, and/or the role of psychological stress, the jury nevertheless is still out as to how sport violence should be handled. Small wonder, then, that concussions continue to be diagnosed, the lucrative Super Bowl being the crowning example of mixing hoopla with horrendously sanctioned violence. The NFL has eased marijuana restrictions for players, and it is also encouraging that head trauma research has intensified. "Fearing a shrinking pipeline of new players and fans," Ken Belson (2022) has nevertheless noted, "the NFL has spent hundreds of millions of dollars to assuage nervous parents that the game can be made safer."

The Culture of Football Violence

> Professional football…interlinks four qualities that drive the American violence machine: physical brutality, profit-maximizing commercialism, an authoritarian-military mentality and sexism.
>
> —Eugene Bianchi, "The Super Bowl Culture of Male Violence." (1974)

The culture of sport violence is certainly not a new one, James Surowiecki (2019) writing this about the NFL on the occasion of its hundredth anniversary:

"The NFL has never stopped changing. But a few things remain constant, including the league's popularity and brutality." Like military institutions, sporting ones emphasize hyper-masculinity that call on participants to "man up," to act "like a man," to "be manly" in word and deed at any and all costs (Butterworth 2008). "In the age of drones, football is war between individual men," Michael Mandelbaum (2020) asserts. "Field generals. Captains. Gunslingers. Blitzes and bullets and bombs," Bauer (2020), has mused, adding, "From winning the battle in the trenches to protecting your territory to defending the home field, football drips with references to war. And the NFL has taken full advantage." Concomitant with that, fans can claim that they want safer football, but in truth they savor the hard-hitting combat of the gridiron—witness how it deals with helmets. Nevertheless, consider the flyovers that occur over Super Bowls (recent Air Force bombers being a trio called The Warzone), patriotic flags, performances by Armed Forces bands and service members participating in choruses and as color guards, and of course the National Anthem. "Athletes—both amateur and professional, who wear gimmicky uniforms to promote inclusiveness, patriotism, and/or sponsorship opportunities—are common sights on sporting fields and in arenas and stadia," Molly Yanity (2021, 76) has noted. "Since September 11, 2001, athletes and fans performing patriotic rituals in military-themed uniforms have become expected at sporting events." Think camouflage jerseys. Or, consider this interpretation of the most recent Super Bowl (Blanco 2021):

> While Jazmine Sullivan and Eric Church belted out the National Anthem, viewers saw images of military personnel stationed in Kuwait wearing their camouflage. NFL players and coaches, hands over their hearts, turned toward the flag. The song came to an end with fireworks and the familiar military flyover. Three Air Force bombers conducted a "first-of-its-kind" trifecta flyover… Highlighting the military is not a new thing for the National Football League. From surprise homecomings and on-field enlistment ceremonies, to members of various military outfits singing "God Bless America," to flyovers, the NFL has a long history of draping itself in the flag. What you may not know is that the Department of Defense has paid them for it.

The Case of Pat Tillman

> The American media are like tired old dogs, dutifully fetching official lies on command and dropping them like bones at the feet of an unsuspecting public. We in turn reward them by buying both the products and the myths they sell us. Eventually, however, the products fail and the myths unravel. When the

government's popularity wanes sufficiently, despite the support of a compliant press, even old dogs can come up with new tricks, reviving the lost art of investigative reporting.

—Michael I. Niman, "Who Killed Pat Tillman?" (2006)

With all the attention to the role of the military in this discussion, it behooves us to recall, with respect, Pat Tillman (1976–2004). Although the closest he actually came to participating in a Super Bowl was XLVI/2012 when his retired #40 Arizona Cardinals jersey was displayed at the NFL Experience, Tillman is remembered for forfeiting his NFL of $3.6M to enlist in the US Army, serving first in Iraq and then being killed in Afghanistan. Soon after being granted hero status by the Bush administration, however, his death took on the tenor of controversy when it was disclosed as being the result of "friendly fire"—a revelation picked up by both the Tillman family and critics of the war for the fact that the Department of Defense delayed the disclosure as a means of protecting its military image. "They lied when Tillman died," his brother Kevin said in testimony before the Committee on Oversight and Government Reform' s 2007 "Misleading Information from the Battlefield" hearing. Arguing that 9/11 prompted American sports to exploit a culture of war, Dave Zirin (2011) stated: "The sports arena has been an organizer of patriotism, a recruiter for the US armed forces, and at times a funhouse mirror, reflecting the principles of freedom in a manner so misshapen and distorted as to rise to the level of farce." Word was, Pat Tillman loved his country and wanted to fight its enemy. *Sports Illustrated* detailed his sense of destiny to do the right thing, his modesty, how *Braveheart* and *Saving Private Ryan* were among his favorite films, and how he loved America so much that, following the World Trade Center disaster of 9/11, he simply had to follow his heart. Yet, for too long, his censored fratricide involved convoluted controversies and cover-ups. Pat's brother Kevin, who also enlisted and who was on duty when told Pat died heroically in combat with Taliban fighters, later went bitterly public with his denunciation of the wars and his disillusionment with the Bush administration's alleged threats to America, its claims about weapons of mass destruction, suggestions that Iraq was linked to the 9/11 attacks, and the declaration that the underlying purpose of the war was the establishment of democracy. In particular, he focused on the secrets: secret prisons, secret kidnappings, secret detentions without charges, secret tortures. Here is some of his powerful rhetoric:

- Somehow American leadership, whose only credit is lying to its people and illegally invading a nation, has been allowed to steal the courage, virtue, and honor of its soldiers on the ground.
- Somehow those afraid to fight an illegal invasion decades ago are allowed to send soldiers to die for an illegal invasion they started.
- Somehow faking character, virtue, and strength is tolerated.
- Somehow profiting from tragedy and horror is tolerated.
- Somehow the death of tens, if not hundreds of thousands of people is tolerated.
- Somehow torture is tolerated.
- Somehow lying is tolerated.
- Somehow a narrative is more important than reality…

On March 4, 2006, the U.S. Defense Department Inspector General ordered a criminal investigation into Tillman's death, wanting to determine whether it was the result of negligent homicide. Aware that the military code should provide clear guidance relative to information about soldiers' death, they were left to wonder what script should be believed. There is quite a legacy: the tax-exempt Pat Tillman Foundation (www.pattillmanfoundation.org), Team Tillman's many causes, a memorial at Sun Devil Stadium and a memorial bridge bearing Pat Tillman's name around the Hoover Dam, his (San Jose, CA) high school football field (re)named for him, the Pat Tillman Scholarship at Lincoln Law School of San Jose, Pat Tillman Freedom Plaza at State Farm Stadium in Glendale, AZ, the "Pat Tillman Memorial Tunnel" entering Sun Devil Stadium at the University of Arizona, an annual Pat's Run fundraiser, and much more. If he was a reluctant hero (Staurowsky 2009), Pat Tillman as picture-perfect poster boy/propaganda tool of the Pentagon continues to be usurped. His story, in microcosm, manipulated as it was by the media, exemplifies so many strategies and truths about the military and its surrounding jargon. For more information, check out the following: Mike Fish's four-part series for ESPN.com: *An Un-American Tragedy* for ESPN.com; Mary Tillman's 2008 book *Boots on the Ground by Dusk: My Tribute to Pat Tillman*; *The Tillman Fratricide* (July 2008)—report of Henry Waxman's House Oversight and Government Reform Committee; Jon Krakauer's *Where Men Win Glory: The Odyssey of Pat Tillman* (2009); and *The Tillman Story*, a 2010 documentary by director Amir Bar-Lev that premiered at the Sundance Film Festival. Pat Tillman made it clear from the start that he never wanted to be considered a hero or to be used for propaganda purposes. Monitoring the political discourse surrounding his hijacked case study allows us to honor him in our own way.

GBV and the Super Bowl

> Whether or not there's some sick synergy on Super Sunday between beer, betting and beatings, between violence on the field and violence in the home, there is good reason to bring this issue into the national spotlight on this particular day.
>
> —Anna Quindlen, *Time to Tackle This* (January 17, 1993)

First, it behooves us to include some definitions and descriptions. Variously called spousal or intimate partner abuse and/or battering, domestic violence most often takes place against women (one in four in the United States)—and so we use the term "gender-based violence" (GBV) for acts that might be physical, psychological, sexual, even economic. Article 1(5) of the Sexual Violence Protocol defines it as "any act which violates the sexual autonomy and bodily integrity of women and children under international criminal law," including but not limited to the following: rape, sexual assault, grievous bodily harm, assault or mutilation of female reproductive organs, sexual slavery, enforced prostitution, forced pregnancy, enforced sterilization, harmful practices, sexual exploitation, trafficking, enslavement, forced abortions or pregnancies, infections with sexually transmitted diseases, and "any other act or form of sexual violence of comparable gravity." NFL players, Benjamin Morris (2014a, 2014b), has pointed out, "have been particularly prone to domestic violence arrests," a factor that is particularly worrisome due to their hyper-visibility and celebrity status.

Reporting how a coalition of groups, under the umbrella of the watchdog group Fairness and Accuracy in Reporting (FAIR), was requesting the Super Bowl network to air public service spots on the phenomenon of domestic violence, Anna Quindlen was one of the first journalists to encourage the public to see the correlation: "The football game story is omnipresent: the kids make too much noise during a crucial play, or someone steps in front of the screen, or he loses a bet, or he runs out of beer, and 'Pow!' " Based on reports and pleas from shelter workers that this is the busiest day of the year, her insights reached a large population.

In 1993, Robert Lipsyte wrote in *New York Times* about what he labeled the "Abuse Bowl"—an almost inevitable post-game result of battered women relative to televised football. "Violence doesn't excite us, and that's what is going on in football," Mariah Burton Nelson wrote the next year, adding that, "Football represents a world where men are strong, men are violent, men are worshipped. And women are absent, or sex objects." Her insights have been helpful to what some pundits came to call a "Day of Dread," with reports that women's shelters and hotlines are busier on Super Sunday than any other day of the year. As time went on, while some disputed rampant spousal abuse, the networks produced a PSA declaring that "Domestic violence is a crime," and one study reported a 40 percent increase in "wife beating." Family law Attorney Carl O. Graham (2019) points out that "The NFL has had plenty of well-earned notoriety for its domestic violence over the years. Throw testosterone, alcohol, and emotional fans into the mix, and this link between the Super Bowl and domestic violence was certainly easy to believe"—and yet, he calls the association a false narrative. The saddest conclusion is that toxic masculinity is actually a much more frequent occurrence, albeit heightened by a holiday mood.

There has been a rash of outings about football players gone foul that make New York Jets' quarterback Michael Vick's dogfighting story pale by comparison. Consider:

- In 2000, Rod Smith, a wide receiver with the Denver Broncos, reportedly beat his live-in girlfriend, the mother of his two children, by banging her head on the floor and choking her.
- Linebacker Robert Reynolds of the Tennessee Titans was arrested in 2006 on domestic and assault charges relating to his now ex-wife, as well as later reports of criminal damage and disorderly conduct relative to his little boy.
- Dallas Cowboy wide receiver Dez Bryant was arrested in 2012 on a Class A misdemeanor domestic violence charge over an incident with his mother.
- A. J. Jefferson, Minnesota Vikings cornerback, was arrested in 2013 on a felony count of domestic assault by strangulation of her 23-year-old girlfriend.
- Just three days after the NFL's announcement against domestic violence, Ray McDonald, defensive end for the San Francisco 49ers, was arrested in 2016 for domestic violence as a felony.
- Another defensive end—Greg Hardy of the Carolina Panthers—was convicted of assaulting his former girlfriend (he threw her on a pile of shotguns) and threatening to kill her.

- Running back Adrian Peterson of the Minnesota Vikings was charged with child abuse after whipping his 4-year-old son with a tree branch, then barred from all team activities until the case is resolved.
- Arizona Cardinals running back Jonathan Dwyer pleaded not guilty to aggravated assault after breaking his wife's nose.
- In November 2021, Minnesota Vikings running back Dalvin Cook was accused of violently assaulting his girlfriend; he claimed he was the victim even though he admitted to cheating on her while she was hospitalized after miscarrying their child.

And then there is the case of Baltimore Ravens running back Raymell Mourice ("Ray") Rice, who became the poster boy of domestic violence when he was caught on camera on Valentine's Day 2014 knocking his then-fiancé Janay Palmer unconscious in a casino elevator (Fuller 2015). Initially, the NFL simply gave him a slap on the wrist of a $529,411 fine and a suspension of two weeks and allowed to keep his $44M/year ($129M for the last two years, with bonuses included) contract. As the video of the attack went viral, however, NFL Commissioner Roger Goodell brought the topic of this form of "unnecessary roughness" into the sporting mainstream, and soon Ray Rice was part of the #WhyILeft movement.

Steve Bisciotti, Ravens owner, issued a letter of apology to season ticket holders, sponsors, and fans. For weeks, Goodell claimed he had not seen the graphic, incriminating video, which infuriated fans and garnered Bill Simmons of ESPN a three-week suspension when he called the Commissioner a liar on his Grandland. com podcast. Many calls were issued for Goodell's resignation ("#GoodellMustGo")—some by members of Congress, but all he did was to announce that there would be an "independent investigation," headed by former FBI director Robert S. Mueller who was now with WilmerHale—the law firm that negotiated the NFL's $12B deal with DirecTV. Ever aware of its image, the NFL put in-house Anna Isaacson into a newly created post of VP of social responsibility and hired three female outside "senior advisers": Lisa Friel, former head of the NY County District Attorney's Sex Crimes Prosecution United; Jane Randel, cofounder of No More, a domestic violence awareness group; and Rita Smith, former executive director of the National Coalition Against Domestic Violence. It also has made a pledge of support for the Domestic Violence Hotline and announced the launch of educational programs on sexual violence and domestic abuse prevention for all of the NFL's thirty-two teams. Although much of the media considered

his actions a sincere start, I must admit that, watching Goodell's public appearance in September 2014—after nine days of anticipation, some sports columnists
accusing him of hiding in his bunker—he struck me as very smug. Even during
the Q&A he notably called on male reporters and then was most condescending
to the few females present. Also, it really made me laugh when the Commissioner
announced that the NFL's "new personal conduct policies" were to be implemented by the time of the Super Bowl; it felt like product placement for a day that has
become the country's unofficial national holiday. My attention to sponsorship
was prompted by news of some corporate loyalists who threatened to sever ties;
in particular, as reported by *Christian Science Monitor* (Axelrad 2014), "Procter
& Gamble most recently pulled its brand of Crest toothpaste out of the league's
campaign for breast cancer awareness month. That came after Anheuser-Busch
(midway through a six-year, $1.2B deal), McDonald's, and Visa all issued crit-
ical statements of the league and Nike suspended its endorsement contract with
Peterson." "I am a mother, a wife, and a passionate football fan," began Indra
Nooyi, CEO of PepsiCo, before adding that domestic violence in the world of
professional football is "disgusting, absolutely unacceptable," and that the NFL's
mishandling of the issue cast a cloud over its integrity (McGregor 2014).

Not surprisingly, Ray Rice appealed, was reinstated, and then became a free
agent. Sadly, but realistically, it must be noted that as his saga unfolded, television
ratings remained high—sometimes even rising. "Amid the images and reports of
battered women and children, there may finally be consensus that NFL games are
superfluous," declared John Branch (2009), adding "that the standings matter less
than the blotter, bruises and brain scans. But the games go on as scheduled, as if
nothing happened, no matter how far the league veers wildly off script." The Ms.
Foundation suggested that the NFL adopt non-sexist advertising; pay its cheerleaders decent wages; promote and hire female coaches, referees, and sportscasters;
and generally include more women of color throughout its executive offices. Chris
B. Geyerman (2016) has called the Ray Rice case remarkable, pointing out how it
featured as a top story in NBC News' Year in Review; using Frame Analysis, he
discusses how domestic violence is an NFL problem as well as a relational one:

> The rhetorical strategies used by the NFL in its response to the media framing
> of domestic violence as an NFL problem allowed the NFL to reposition itself as
> part of a solution to the problem. This repositioning resulted in large part from
> two themes that characterize this frame: the competence of NFL Commissioner
> Roger Goodell and the NFL's newfound recognition that domestic violence is a
> complex and pervasive social problem.

From a GCDA point of view, we see how "deinstitutionalizing" and/or de-gendering a problem might remove it from exactly the people (in this case, abused women) who most need it recognized (see Berns 2001).

During the second quarter of Super Bowl XLIX/2015, a PSA on domestic violence called NO MORE aired before its largest audience to date: 114.4 viewers. The groundbreaking thirty-second chilling presentation simply had a woman on a telephone calling 911 with a pizza order, dispatchers fortunately figuring out what was really going on in the address she had given. The NFL pledged $5M/year for five years to the National Domestic Violence Hotline, and calls to the hotline reportedly have spiked ever since, ClearTicket.com reporting as recently as 2019 a staggering eighty current and former NFL players arrested for domestic violence a combined ninety-four times. With O. J. Simpson cited for a Dishonorable Mention, the list includes twenty-six who were members of Super Bowl–winning teams and that, "As for their victims, 13 had at least one child with their assailant and six were pregnant at the time of the abuse."

Washington Post columnist George Will (January 26, 2016), who first cites the research about a surge in car accidents after the Super Bowl and then pooh-poohs it as a myth, feels the same way about gender-based violence (GBV) and the Games ("So-called experts blamed provocatively dressed cheerleaders for turning men into testosterone-crazed brutes"), and he is just as snarky about the concussion issue. Still, he makes an interesting point: "Football's kinetic energy is increasing as the players become bigger and even the biggest become faster. In 1980, only three NFL players weighed 300 or more pounds. This season, 354 did" (January 9, 2019).

Reviewing the historical persistence of brutality in pro football, Stephen H. Norwood (2019, 62) points out that "The ability to both mete out physical punishment, and take it without flinching, has remained central to football in more than a century." Playing while injured is expected, painkillers routinely administered without question, and of course opioid addiction is a fear. Getting "dinged," then losing all memory of it is routine. Face masks, introduced by the NFL in the mid-1950s "to reduce the number of facial injuries like broken cheekbones, broken noses, eye damage, and loss of teeth" (64), at least have been accepted, and scandals about bounties for knocking players off the field (known as "cart-offs"—part of BountyGate) have been unearthed and punished. Michael Real (1995, 115) summarizes it best: "American football is an aggressive, strictly regulated team game fought between males who use both violence and technology to win monopoly control of property for the economic gain of individuals within a nationalistic, entertainment context."

Perhaps we all should wear the purple bows denoting Domestic Violence Awareness 24/7 because, as this is being written the 2021 NFL draft profiling a top recruit gave as one of his key traits the fact that this good, competitive blitzer has "good explosiveness," "willingness to play through pain," and "is a good tackler with an appetite for violence." Recognizing how the Super Bowl is "a major event in many American households with all of the fanfare, planning, and preparation of any other holiday," Gantz, Wang, and Bradley (2006, 379) point out how it represents our holiday-related expectations. Contrarily, they suggest, "It appears that when one throws together a mix of people, expectations, anxiety, and alcohol—and in many locales, in close quarters under wintry conditions—a same and next day spike in violence is the result." Take this as a warning, not an urban legend.

Health Issues

As the big day approaches, fans and players alike experience various forms of stress, from thinking about preparations to general overdoing. Hearts race in anticipation, sometimes leading to heart attacks and/or significant indigestion. Overeating is a given. Team loyalty can be extreme.

In 2017, Dearing et al. studied 196 heavy drinkers, about equally men and women, with an average age of 36, and found men drank much more than the women on Super Bowl Sunday. Part of a hazardous syndrome known as "celebratory drinking," the idea of anticipating festivity adds to lowered self-control.

When, on November 3, 2021, Green Bay Packers quarterback Aaron Rodgers tested positive for COVID-19, the sports world's initial response was one of surprise, since Rodgers had claimed he was "immunized." When it was revealed, however, that he had taken an alternative treatment of the anti-parasitic drug ivermectin, he began to bash the "woke mob" that criticized him, claiming that body autonomy and ability should be an individual decision. "Some of the rules to me are not based in science at all," Rodgers claimed on *The Pat McAfee Show* after being tested positive, before a mandatory ten-day quarantine forcing him to miss one game. "They are based purely in trying to out and shame people, like needing to wear a mask at a podium when everyone in the room is vaccinated and wearing a mask makes no sense to me." Although Rodgers never acknowledged that he might have been wrong, he drew enormous criticism from sportscaster Bob

Costas and FanSided's Matt Lombardo for his selfishness, NFL Network's Michael Irvin slamming his dishonesty, NFL analyst Terry Bradshaw sharing deep disappointment, and Hall of Fame coach Jimmy Johnson saying, "I respect his attitude toward being an individual. But this is a team game." Other reactions were that Rodgers was just lucky. Toward the end of the season, the NFL tightened its COVID-19 protocols, recommending that players and their families be vaccinated, demanding that people wear masks in team facilities, and that testing continue. While some 94 percent of players, coaches, and staff were reported as vaccinated, the fact that the Packers were fined $300,000 for failing to monitor whether players were adhering to guidelines no doubt played a part in overall attitudes about Aaron Rodgers' gnostic stance.

Football Lingo

The football playing field is loaded with sexual metaphors; starting at the 10-yard line you might be holding hands, hugging at the 20, kissing on the check at 30, the lips at 40. By midfield come tongues, and eventually you might get to the goal line. *Kick-off* is asking for a date, *kicking it deep* is asking a virgin for a date, an *on-sides kick* is asking a slut out for a date, and the *kick return* connotes how far you got on the date. Beyond this introduction, you can no doubt figure out what a *fumble* is, or a *down*, a *turnover*, a *rain delay, missed field goal*, or *running with the ball*, even *passing plays*. Keep using your imagination to figure out differences between offense and defense strategies, as well as penalties.

The Language of the Super Bowl

As early as 1981, Nancy Theberge critiqued sports as "a fundamentally sexist institution that is male dominated and masculine in orientation" (342), and since then a number of researchers have added fodder to this argument (Connell and Messerschmidt 2005; Davis 1997; Messner 1992, 1997, 2002; Messner and Sabo 1990; Nelson 1994). For male football fans, there are always cheerleaders to encourage infantile behavior, the single sideline female reporter who can be critiqued, players' wives who take on celebrity status, and advertisements feeding into patriarchal norms. In addition to "man talk," militarism, patriotism, and blatant sexism, Super Bowl rhetoric is loaded with subtexts of violence. Without even outlining war-like and sexist football lingo, consider this from my 2009 publication about football rhetoric:

Strategically, the goal of American football seems pretty basic: eleven players on each team, *offense* or *defense*, try to reach *end zones* where they can *score*. The team with the most points wins. The *ball*, sometimes (erroneously) referred to as a pigskin, is handled by a *ballcarrier*, who hopes to keep it away from *ball hawks*. So, there might be *body blocking, butt-blocking, chop blocking, power blocking, roughing a kicker or passer, ball-stripping, zone blocking, flea-flicking, spiking, encroaching* or *eating the ball*. A player might be a *headhunter, a heavy hitter, a sledgehammer, a jumper, a monster, a punishing runner*, or a *punter*. Opponents are always on the lookout for weak sides. He might deliberately spear a fellow player's helmet, make a *sucker play, sack or shank the ball, make a plunge*, or *tackle a ballcarrier*. There are even some ghoulish terms, a *coffin corner* being one of four

places where sidelines and goal lines intersect, a *dead ball* one out of play and *dead-man (or sleeper) play* referring to an illegal pretense for passing. A *dying quail*, when a toss lacks speed and power, can also be called a *duck ball*. *Skull sessions*, also known as chalk talk, review and predict plays. At the other extreme, how does one explain that football lingo also includes "Hail Mary," a low-percentage desperation pass that appeals to a higher power for completion. It may not surprise you that there can be *intentional grounding, intercepts, slashing, "unsportsmanlike conduct,"* and a *disabled list*. Or that *possession* is of prime importance. (180)

"If there are people at your party who don't know shit about football, they better fucking all be women," declares Drew Magary (2009). Welcome to the Old Boys Club. If you're feeling offended, he later adds "No fucking kids. No kids fucking."

Football Media Relative to the Super Bowl

Football has been fictionalized in only a few books, the best-known being Robert Daley's *Only a Game* (1967), Don DeLillo's *End Zone* (1972), Peter Gent's *North Dallas Forty* (1973), Dan Jenkins' *Semi-Tough* (1977), Frank Deford's *Everybody's All-American* (1981), and Michael Lewis' *The Blind Side: Evolution of a Game* (2007). Don DeLillo's 2020 *The Silence* is set on Super Sunday 2022, as one of the characters turns to that habit even though a digital apocalypse comes to turn out the big game. There are wonderful nonfiction ones, like Derrick Coleman Jr.'s *No Excuses: Growing Up Deaf and Achieving My Super Bowl Dreams* (2015), Michael Bennett's *Things That Make White People Uncomfortable* (2018), and so many more listed in the appendices. Buzz Bissinger's nonfiction bestseller *Friday Night Lights: A Town, a Team, and a Dream* (1990) deserves special attention here, as it shows how much football means to Texas and Texans and was made into both a television series and a 2004 movie.

By way of a literature review, the closest thing to this book historically, if limited only to that aspect, are Rozelle and Didinger's 1990 *The Super Bowl: Celebrating a Quarter-Century of America's Greatest Game,* or *Sports Illustrated Gold: 50 Years of the Big Game* (2015), although both are more photo- and reference-oriented than this volume. Bill Polian's *Super Bowl Blueprints* (2021) sticks to football champion dynasties.

Only a few football books have been made into movies, such as *Paper Lion* (1968, with Alan Alda), *Semi-Tough* (1977, with Burt Reynolds), *North Dallas Forty* (1979, with Nick Nolte), *Everybody's All-American* (1988), with Dennis Quaid); never mind that there are more than one hundred football films (Fuller 2009a). The forty-seven-minute comedy *Super Bowl,* a behind-the-scenes "documentary" of Super Bowl X/1976 between the Pittsburgh Steelers and Dallas Cowboys, featuring Christopher Guest and Bill Murray, appeared the same year as the cheesy disaster movie *Two-Minute Warning* ("91,000 People. 33 Exit Gates…One Sniper"). John Frankenheimer's thriller *Black Sunday* the next year was expected to be a mega-blockbuster, influenced as it was by the 1972 Munich Olympics, but it ended up being a bit too political and psychologically complex for the movie-going public. The NFL has produced numerous films—backstories of winning teams, players, coaches, plus highlights of specific games from the archives in addition to its annual release of *America's Game: The Super Bowl Champions.* While you may count the 2015 biographical film *Concussion,* the best stuff probably still are the trailers.

The 1992 sport comedy *Necessary Roughness,* about a 34-year-old quarterback's return to college football, is that basic story about underdog losers who have to come together as a team for the classic comeback. Starring Scott Bakula, Hector Elizondo, Robert Loggia, as well as Sinbad, directed by Stan Dragoti, it featured the Texas State Armadillos and had cameos by football pros Dick Butkus, Ben Davidson, Bubba Smith, Earl Campbell, Roger Craig, Tony Dorsett, Ed "Too Tall" Jones, Randy White, Jim Kelly, Jerry Rice, and Herschel Walker as well as sportscaster Chris Berman. Centering around a "death penalty" predicament, everything changes when a woman (model Kathy Ireland, who kicks one of the dudes in the crotch) joins the team and success is theirs— well, after a faked point. Texas Monthly (O'Neal 2021) has declared that "*Necessary Roughness* was among the first movies to probe Texas's unique, slightly unhealthy football obsession, even as it also mocked us as a bunch of redneck hicks."

Oliver Stone's 1999 film *Any Given Sunday*, subtitled "Life Is a Contact Sport," remains of the best examples of football as battle by modern-day gladiators. Referring to when Americans mostly tune in the game, it begins with a quotation from Coach Vince Lombardi exalting those lying "exhausted on the field of battle" before moving into a super-charged plot about coaches and players and the frenetic activities both on and off the field. Deliberately "R" rated, it contained offensive language, lots of violence, sexuality, and even full-frontal male nudity amidst bone-crushing injuries, thunderous sounds, and much profanity. Men dominate not only the playing of football but also its economics and politics, serving as photographers for nearly naked cheerleaders, purveyors of sexual services, doctors, and others of authority while a player named Shark is seen snorting a line of cocaine off a woman's breast. Product placement includes Budweiser beer, cars (Mercedes, GMC trucks, Jaguars, Ford Explorers), computers, even WWF programming. The argument could be made, in fact, that the title could have been "Any Given Advertisement"; it was so packed with commercials. Polo, Armani, Hugo Boss, Fubu, Levi's, and Reebok labels were not even subtle, and at one point, Reebok shoes fit into a plot whereby L.L. Cool J. as a running back worn them to break a 2,000-yard rushing record. Cell phones from Motorola and Nokia were prominent, Macanudo cigars puffed for celebrations. Even media was on display: *Forbes* framed, *Sports Illustrated* on the furniture, and *Time* part of a conversation. While Queen's "We will rock you" resounded while Apple, Adidas, Pepsi, IBM, First Union Bank, Bacardi, Excel helmets, Sprint, Sony, Tag, Telex headphones, Toyota, Home Depot, DMX, VO-5, Old Spice, Right Guard, All Sport, Nikon cameras, Lay's chips, Mr. Peanuts, Poland Springs, even MET-REX were inserted into the film. Women were either drunks or dominatrixes, epitomized by Cameron Diaz a tough-as-nails team owner/inheritor, others either prostitutes or simple partyers. Few were articulate, and most conversations were laced with swear words or sexy statements such as "Don't act like a pussy," "Fuck us up," "Kick some butt," or "Be a complete prick." Perhaps this was the worst: "We win, we penetrate, we win."

Relative to televised programs about football, ESPN's *Playmakers*, which premiered on August 26, 2003, provides a fascinating study of the role of the NFL's self-imaging/promotion (Fuller 2004). The eleven-part series began with an enormous promotional campaign, one reporter calling them "saturation-level promos."

Playmakers had its own web page, billing itself as a "critically acclaimed drama" with an overview reading: "ESPN's Original Entertainment's first-ever dramatic series is a gritty ensemble chronicling the behind-the-scenes and off-the-field lives of the players, families, coaches and owner of a fictional professional football team." Filmed on location in Toronto, centered around a fictional professional football team called the Cougars, *Playmakers* made media history by introducing America's favorite sport in a new format. If the idea was to deal with "reality" relative to pro football, the series might be said to have scored an instant touchdown, but one that worked more like a boomerang. True to its stated decision to be a gritty gridiron profile, those topics included everything ranging from drug use to domestic violence, injuries to criminal intent, hidden homophobia to open racism, and the politics inherent in team play, team ownership, coaching, and corporate controls. In essence, it was a male soap opera, a guilty pleasure for many men who didn't like to admit how much they liked it, never mind that they watched it at all.

From a sociocultural perspective, it becomes increasingly clear that football in general and the Super Bowl particularly continue to evolve as forces relative to demographics such as fandom, racism, gender, ethnicity, and even religion and rhetoric. Factor in other issues such as violence, health, language, and cinematic representation, and it becomes easier to see what a complex topic is America's game. "Is it coincidence that America is the strongest, richest and most vibrant society, and also the sole country whose national sport is gridiron football?...Football both expresses the American spirit and plays a role in that spirit," Gregg Easterbrook prefaces his 2013 book *The King of Sports*. He argues that football essentially is built on a "plantation mentality," poor inner-city, rural players at the bottom of that pile. The Super Bowl, who must remain reminded, is the penultimate aspect of football.

As the significance of sport continues to be (re)interpreted by serious scholarship we see the importance of examining intersectionalities in sport relative to racism, gender, ethnicity, religion, and more—especially, underlined by language. We live in an era when words like BIPOC (Black, Indigenous or other people of color), POC (Person of color), and gender-neutral terms like Latinx are interspersed with terms like *white privilege, cancel culture*, and *critical race theory* (CRT). As a platform for promoting equities and empowering athletes and audiences alike, the Super Bowl as media sport and rhetorical vehicle makes for an ideal case study.

## CHAPTER 5

Parties Celebrating the Super Bowl

The Super Bowl is outsized, preposterous, excessive…(It) is just a big, over-done party.

—Greg Easterbrook, "Don't Analyze That: A Day of
Excess Won't Kill Us." (2005)

For millions of people, whether football fans or not, the Super Bowl has long been an excuse to gather at a bar or restaurant or in someone's living room to party, eat food that is not remotely healthy, throw back some beer or cocktails and laugh at the commercials. Some even pay attention to the game.

—Julie Cresswell, "Super Bowl Means Snacking, Even
without Parties." (2021)

Super Bowl Sunday may be the most widely celebrated entertaining day of the year. It's nondenominational…

—*Super Bowl party with Todd English* (epicurious.com)

Party on!

The Super Bowl party is inextricably tied to the televised Super Bowl, a pre-dominantly American unofficial holiday, (with) parties typically held in private homes and in commercial bars, clubs, and taverns. Such parties are devoted to watching the game, eating and drinking, and chatting during commercial breaks and during slow moments of the game. Licensing fees restrict the use of the term Super Bowl for commercial purposes so bars and clubs often refer to Super Bowl events in marketing materials as "watching the big game."

—Adamson and Segan, *Entertaining from Ancient Rome
to the Super Bowl* (2008, 480)

Don't discount the parties, whether in home, bars, stadiums, arenas, theatres, restaurants, hotels, convention centers or—depending on the location and the weather—in back yards. Some are lavish tailgates, some simple barstool-gates, while others are plentiful potlucks, or picnics, and/or just general pig-outs. Even that first Super Bowl 1/1967 had a Commissioner's Party (Frommer 2015). The mid-winter timing is ideal, as we have just come off a holiday season and are ready to break dieting resolutions and to party. Madison Avenue and constant media hype also help. But be warned: Super Bowl parties can be very costly, CNBC (El-Bawab 2021) reporting that, according to the National Retail Federation (NRF), Americans spend an average of $81 per person or a total of $14.8B. From a survey of 7,000 adults in early January—before teams were announced, nearly 61M said they planned to attend a party, 44M said they would be hosting a party, and 13M said they would be watching the game at a bar. Remember: We consume more on this day than any other than Thanksgiving, and there hardly exists a fan who needs to be food-bribed. At Fort Bragg, NC, where cooks need to prepare for 15,000 US troops, a food supervisor reports: "Thanksgiving is our Super Bowl. And we can't lose."

If you want to consult some cookbooks, let me recommend the following: David Bowers' *The Ultimate Sports Fans Cookbook: Festive Recipes for Inside the Home and Outside the Stadium* (Skyhorse 2014); Candy Coleman's *Pigskin Picnics* (CC Enterprises 1980); Ray "Dr. BBQ" Lampe's *The NFL Gameday Cookbook* (Chronicle 2008).

On-site fans start partying the Thursday before the game, so for Super Bowl L111/2019 that meant beginning with a Music Fest with performances by Atlanta's Ludacris, Migos, Lil Yachty, Lil Baby, Lil Jon, Ciara, Metro Boomin and twenty-one Savage—ticket prices being $75. Double that for Friday, headlined by Aerosmith and Post Malone, and then $400 on Saturday for shows with Bruno Mars and Cardi B. What used to be exclusive is becoming more open and more lucrative. "Shaq's Fun House" party featured Migos, Diplo, Tiesto, Lil Jon, T-Pain, and DJ Irie, costing $2,100 for a standing ticket in the VIP table and $550 for a meet and greet with the host. *Sports Illustrated*'s party had Snoop Dogg and Lil Wayne and fans wanting to cozy up to celebrities paid $2,500 to $25,000 for a ten-person VIP table. Maxim's pregame party entry fee was $1,250, Flo Rida's "Leather & Laces" $1,500, and the entry for Maxim's "Big Game Experience Party," hosted by Jaime Foxx, Future, Diplo, and DJ Ruckus, went for $3,500. South Beach lives to party, so, for Super Bowl L1V/2020, the CBSSports.com reported these hot parties, places, and people:

- SiriusXM & Pandora Opening Drive Super Concert Series, The Fillmore Miami Beach at The Jackie Gleason Theater; **Guests:** The Chainsmokers, Lizzo
- Bud Light Super Bowl Music Fest, American Airlines Arena; **Guests:** DJ Khaled, Meek Mill, Maroon 5, Dan + Shay, Snoop Dogg, Guns N' Roses
- Planet Pepsi Zero Sugar with Harry Styles, Meridian at Island Gardens
- Shaq's Fun House, Mana Wynwood Convention Center; **Guests:** Shaquille O'Neal, Diddy, Diplo, Pitbull, Tiesto
- Delano Live Presented by TIDAL; **Guest:** Lil Wayne
- Bootsy on the Water; **Guest:** Post Malone
- Leather & Laces, Soho Studios; **Guests:** Lil Jon, Snoop Dogg
- Gronk Beach, North Beach Bandshell; **Guests:** Rob Gronkowski, Diplo, Kaskade, Rick Ross, Flo Rida
- *Sports Illustrated*'s "The Party," Fontainebleau Miami Beach; **Guests:** DaBaby, Black Eyed Peas, Marshmello
- AT&T TV Super Saturday Night, Meridian at Island Gardens; **Guest:** Lady Gaga
- Rolling Stone Live, SLS South Beach; **Guests:** Ciara, DJ Khaled, Paris Hilton
- Maxim Havana Nights, On the Water at Virginia Key Island; *Guests*: The Chainsmokers, Rick Ross, Lost Kings
- The Players Tailgate Miami, Hard Rock Stadium; **Guests:** Guy Fieri, Charles Woodson
- The first Super Bowl party took place after Super Bowl 1/1967—what was known as the Pepsi Party, sponsored by Pepsi bigwig Samuel Dresch who, with his wife, flew in two private planes of their "closest friends" for the game and afterwards went to Perino's, on Wilshire Boulevard in Los Angeles. Since then, the competition for Best Party is waged between Maxim, Playboy, Madden, and others, depending on the venue(s).

Super Sunday HQ, which bills itself as "the world's #1 influencer & TV media outlet for Super Bowl events since 2007," the "ultimate insider's guide to celebrity Super Bowl events," and the "Access Hollywood" of Super Bowl parties, arranges and reports on star-studded parties and tailgates. Donald Trump's 2020 Super Bowl weekend at Mar-a-Lago was reported to cost taxpayers $3.4M for a weekend trip that included transportation and security costs, golf outings, and a huge party for viewers, including Fox News' Sean Hannity and more than 1,000 women known as the "Trumpettes." CBSSports (Blackburn 2020) listed celebrity parties available in Miami:

- **Party:** SiriusXM & Pandora Opening Drive Super Concert Series, The Fillmore Miami Beach at The Jackie Gleason Theater; **Guests:** The Chainsmokers, Lizzo
- **Party:** Bud Light Super Bowl Music Fest, American Airlines Arena; **Guests:** DJ Khaled, Meek Mill, Maroon 5, Dan + Shay, Snoop Dogg, Guns N' Roses
- **Party:** Planet Pepsi Zero Sugar with Harry Styles, Meridian at Island Gardens
- **Party:** Shaq's Fun House, Mana Wynwood Convention Center; **Guests:** Shaquille O'Neal, Diddy, Diplo, Pitbull, Tiesto
- **Party:** Delano Live Presented by TIDAL; **Guest:** Lil Wayne
- **Party:** Bootsy on the Water; **Guest:** Post Malone
- **Party:** Leather & Laces, Soho Studios; **Guests:** Lil Jon, Snoop Dogg
- **Party:** Gronk Beach, North Beach Bandshell; **Guests:** Rob Gronkowski, Diplo, Kaskade, Rick Ross, Flo Rida
- **Party:** *Sports Illustrated*'s "The Party," Fontainebleau Miami Beach; **Guests:** DaBaby, Black Eyed Peas, Marshmello
- **Party:** AT&T TV Super Saturday Night, Meridian at Island Gardens; **Guest:** Lady Gaga
- **Party:** Rolling Stone Live, SLS South Beach; **Guests:** Ciara, DJ Khaled, Paris Hilton
- **Party:** Maxim Havana Nights, On the Water at Virginia Key Island; **Guests:** The Chainsmokers, Rick Ross, Lost Kings
- **Party:** The Players Tailgate Miami, Hard Rock Stadium; **Guests:** Guy Fieri, Charles Woodson
- **Party:** Pre-Game Party, Hard Rock Stadium; **Guests:** Darius Rucker, NFL stars

But all that frivolity was of course subdued for Super Bowl LV/2021, when COVID-19 put the kibosh on high spirits and "homegating" supplanted tailgating in many places. *New York Times* (Cresswell 2021) cited Carolyn Blocka, a Toronto law clerk and rabid Los Angeles Chargers fan who loves to throw huge buffets but who, this year, sat on a fold-up chair in her garage, door open in 20-

°F weather. Snacks predominated, Frito-Lay producing 70M pounds of product, Buffalo Wild Wings selling more than 11M wings, and DoorDash creating algorithms to predict hour-by-hour demand. It is interesting to note Lydecker et al.'s 2017 study finding that, despite higher prevalence of obesity in Black and Hispanic populations yet low representation of overweight people in commercials, Super Bowl ads for food and beverages nevertheless have racial and ethnic diversity.

Super Bowl Spirits and Munchies

> Perhaps you foolishly think Super Bowl Sunday is a day for celebrating football. Or maybe you are naïve enough to truly believe this is all about love of the game. If so, step away, because real Americans know this about one thing and one thing only: eating disgusting amounts of food. For your country.

> —Jillian Berman, "Americans Eat 1,083,333 Football Fields Worth of Wings on Super Bowl Sunday and Other Fun Facts." (2013)

Buds and brats might be your regular go-tos for Game Day grazing, but it behooves us to consider some of the other standard fare for the day. While there are some 1,410,000 Super Bowl recipes listed on the internet, most of the menu is basically male- and junk food-oriented. You might be interested in some of the staples:

Buffalo Chicken Wings

Buffalo chicken wings, which are de rigueur for Super Bowl parties, actually originated in Buffalo, New York. Word is that, in 1964, Teressa Bellissimo of the Anchor Bar there decided to deep-fry some wings, unbreaded, and then toss them with hot sauce. She served them with celery sticks and blue-cheese dressing, and the wings became so popular that the term Buffalo has come to be synonymous with their flavor. If you want to make your own *Blue Cheese Dip*, mix together 8 oz. cream cheese, 1 minced clove garlic and 1 shallot, 3 tablespoons of milk, ¼ teaspoon cayenne pepper, then 4 oz. crumbled glumps of Roquefort or blue cheese.

Word is that 1.25B chicken wings are consumed on Super Bowl Sunday, along with 12.5M pizzas, 145,000 tons of chips, 4,000 tons of popcorn, and 13.2M pounds of guacamole. Health-conscious fans might try *Sriracha Buffalo Cauliflower Bites*: combine a huge head of cauliflower cut into flowerets with 2 tablespoons olive oil; spread on a large, oiled baking pan, sprinkle with salt and Parmesan cheese, and cook at 450 °F about fifteen minutes. Drizzle with a mixture of 2 tablespoons each Sriracha and hot sauce mixed with 1 tablespoon each melted butter and lemon juice and continue cooking about five minutes more.

Guacamole

According to Marley, The Party Goddess! blog *Vodka & Donuts*, these are the "guac" rules for the Super Bowl:

- Guacamole is THE football party super-food. Of the 1B pounds of avocadoes sold in the United States, 49.5M pounds were consumed on Super Bowl Sunday! *Men's Health* has figured that's enough to fill a football field 12 feet deep.
- The avocado is a fruit, not a vegetable.
- Wholly Guacamole makes the equivalent to over 1,500,000 ice cream scoops per day!
- Football fans across the country will eat more than 80M pounds of avocados, or roughly enough to bury the University of Phoenix Stadium field under 31 feet of the wrinkly-skinned fruit, end zone to end zone.
- According to the Hass Avocado Board, guacamole will account for most of the carnage.

Or, as vice.com ruled it in 2020, "The real winner of the Super Bowl is the avocado industry." Sam Arnold, founder of Denver's The Fort, claims that one of its cooks "discovered" *guac* when he dropped an avocado into some salsa and realized it was irresistible; believe it if you want.

Nachos

Accounting for 29 percent of the (junk?) food consumed on Super Sunday, these tortilla chips—usually covered in melted cheese—have become to Super Bowl what corn candy is to Halloween, turkey to Thanksgiving. Doritos, an American brand of tortilla chips produced by Frito-Lay, decided to do a promo in 2006 called "Crash the Super Bowl" that encouraged viewers to film their own ads featuring the chips, and by 2009 a prize of $1M went to one featuring an office worker fulfilling a prediction that he would get "Free

Doritos" by smashing a vending machine with a crystal ball. When Houston, TX hosted Super Bowl L1/2017, word is that Pico's Mex-Mex Restaurant was extremely popular. Try this unusual *Bacon Hummus* with your nachos: To a 15 oz. can of drained and pureed chickpeas add 8 slices of cooked, chopped bacon, 2 tablespoons each olive oil and lemon juice, 2 finely chopped cloves garlic and salt and pepper to taste.

Submarine Sandwiches

You might call them grinders, or hoagies, heroes, torpedos, po' boys, or other names, but we New Englanders call these cold sandwiches "subs"— after all, the fast-food restaurant franchise called Subway is headquartered in Connecticut. St. Louis has one with a special sauce: Amighetti's. Before they became the Los Angeles Rams, the St. Louis Rams (1995–2015) have had several different homes, but while in Missouri they won Super Bowl XXX1V/1999 beating the Tennessee Titans 23-16. Its next experience, Super Bowl XXXVI/2001, was known for the "Spygate" scandal, the New England Patriots having taped the Rams' walkthrough practice. You cannot lose if you want a sub with Marge Amighetti's winning sauce for subs, which she invented in 1969: Slice some Italian bread lengthwise and load up with ham, roast beef, Genoa salami, cheese, lettuce, tomato, dill pickle slices, sliced sweet onion, and 3 to 4 pepperoncini. Add some of this combination: ½ cup mayonnaise, 3 tablespoons sour cream, 2 tablespoons hot mustard, 1 tablespoon each horseradish, minced green onion, and chopped fresh dill. Combine, mix, and refrigerate for use within several days. Bourbon fans might like *Pork Sandwiches*: Marinate overnight pork tenderloins in ½ cup each of bourbon, soy sauce, brown sugar, and vegetable oil mixed with 6 minced garlics, 2 teaspoons each minced ginger and Worcester sauce, then bake at 425 °F until done (about thirty to forty-five minutes); cool, slice, and serve with mustard.

Chili

"It doesn't matter if your team wins or loses—you have these bowls of chili for comfort" *Bon Appétit* promises as it introduces their favorites, filled with beans, smoky chorizo, squash, and other combos. Still, the Cincinnati Bengals claim theirs is best: 2 chopped onions and 6 clove garlics cooked in 2 tablespoons butter, then 2 lb. ground sirloin, ¼ cup chili powder, 1 teaspoon each cocoa powder, cinnamon, allspice, and cumin added. Cook two minutes then add 2 cups of water, 4 bay leaves, 2 tablespoons each vinegar and honey. Bring to a boil, reduce heat and simmer forty-five minutes and then add 1 can kidney beans and 1 lb. macaroni, 2 tablespoons olive oil, 1 tablespoon butter; cook until al dente. Drain, rise, and serve topped with 2 cups of grated sharp cheddar cheese and 1 cup of diced red onion. Served at the Camp Washington Chili Parlor, which claims "Over 75 years of chili goodness," this Cincinnati landmark had been prominently featured in media and was featured in blues musician Lonnie Mack's *Camp Washington Chili*. Of course, if you want to include meatballs in your buffet, they can serve as a "two-point conversion," as appetizers or entrees.

Peppers Plus

Naturally jalapenos are popular on Super Bowl Sunday, but don't discount fire-roasted peppers and pimento cheese, specialties of North Carolina, who played in XXXVIII/2003 and L/2016. Potato skins might have begun at T.G.I. Friday's in the 1970s, but they still prevail in Louisiana, where New Orleans has hosted the Games eleven times. One of those occasions was Super Bowl XX/1986, when the Chicago Bears defeated the New England Patriots 46-10 and Harry Caray's Italian Steakhouse kept fans happy with meatballs and memorabilia in the restaurant's museum of items collected by the legendary sportscaster. Jalapenos stuffed with sausage are popular: combine 1 pound cooked pork sausage with 8 oz. cream cheese, 1 cup of Parmesan cheese, and 3 tablespoons chopped cilantro, then stuff into 1 pound of peppers and bake at 425 °F for about twenty minutes; serve with Ranch dressing.

Bud

Let's return to that original notion of Bud and brats. Beer and football are so intrinsically considered a team that there are a number of books depicting them: David Nyland's *Beer, Babes, and Balls: Masculinity and Sports Talk Radio* (SUNY 2007); Murray Sperber's *Beer and Circus: How Big-Time Sports Is Crippling Undergraduate Education* (Henry Holt 2000); Larry Wenner and Steve Jackson's *Sport, Beer, and Gender: Promotional Culture and Contemporary Social Life* (Peter Lang 2008). Messner and Montez de Oca (2005) saw ties between advertising for Super Bowls and in *Sports Illustrated* swimsuit issues relative to drawing on "youthful masculinity" to encourage and establish future consumers of various alcoholic beverages. According to ThePostGame.com,

> There's nothing better than a cold brewskie while watching a game. The Super Bowl is no exception; Americans will drink 50M cases of beer on Super Bowl Sunday. Not all beer is created equal, but about 94 percent of beer consumed will be Bud Light, Budweiser, Coors Light, Miller Lite, or Natural Light.

Budweiser has been a fixture, its parent company Anheuser-Busch holding a long-term NFL contract, its mascot Clydesdales familiar even to nondrinkers, and its ads frequent viewer favorites. It has been worth it, winning *USA Today*'s annual Super Bowl Ad Meter survey fourteen times, some favorites being the dog as man's best friend, the one where the dog gives his owner a Bud after they go for a run, or when a guy sitting with his girlfriend gets a call from friends at a bar, drinking Buds, asking him what he's watching and then realizing and ranking on him for not watching football. To go with the brew, Cleveland native celebrity chef Michael Symon suggests beer bratwurst covered with caraway kraut, spicy mustard, and pickles while Houston's Chris Shepherd likes a roast beef sandwich slathered with horseradish cream, pickled red onions, blue cheese, bacon, onion, and tomatoes. Everybody, it turns out, likes *Beer Dip for Pretzels*: Smash together 10 oz. cream cheese, 2 cups shredded cheddar cheese, 1/3 cup beer, an envelope of ranch salad dressing, and an optional dash of cayenne pepper.

O'Donnell and Spires (2008) analyzed Bud Light ads and found that in 2001 the theme was men forced to go shopping with women, in 2003 to listen to women "chat," and in 2004 and 2004 the ads featured women nagging men. In the middle of political debates where Trumpian anti-immigration was a hot topic, it was symbolic that the King of Beers happened to highlight their founder Adolphus Busch's coming to America in the 1850s and the discrimination that he had to overcome. Bud's 2018 "Stand by You" ad had nothing to do with beer but referred to the company's helping victims of nature disasters, while 2019s "Wind Never Felt Better" promoted the company's commitment to clean energy, and more recently it decided not to advertise per se but to support campaigns for COVID-19 vaccines. SaveonBrew.com figures that Super Bowl watchers drive enough beer to fill an Olympic-sized swimming pool nearly two thousand times. Of course, some of your guests might prefer *Margaritas*: 1½ oz. tequila, 1 oz. lime juice, 1½ teaspoon each agave nectar and Grand Marnier; combine in a shaker filled with cracked ice, shake for fifteen seconds, strain, and garnish with a lime wedge. Magary (2009) encourages drinking games where guests take a shot when their quarterback goes down; then again, this is the same guy who decrees that you should "Buy three times the amount of food and alcohol you need" and who implores you to "Have extra cash on hand to cover bets and for cab fare for your friends… don't allow anyone to drive home drunk."

"Grab your favorite Gametime Treats" reads an ad for KitKat, Jolly Rancher Bites, Reese's Peanut Butter Cups, and Hershey's Kisses, and fan favorites always include popcorn, bacon-wrapped weenies, cheese balls, and of course chocolate desserts such as football-shaped brownies. "Food, like sport, is pervasive in Western popular culture," declare Veri and Liberti (2019, 10). "Various food-related issues regularly appear in news reporting—everything from food insecurity to agricultural policies to artisanal trends. We are in an era of the celebrity chef, food memoir, glossy cookbook, and of gastronomic glorification in television, film, and social media."

Planning for Super Bowl Parties

> For many Americans, Super Bowl Sunday isn't about defensive strategy, how the quarterbacks throw or the tantalizing prospect of your favorite team winning a championship ring. It's about the parties.
>
> —Talya Minsberg, "Have Yourself a Ball on Super Bowl Sunday." (2021)

Because it is such a big deal, the hype and hoopla for the Super Bowl begins far in advance of its actual taking place. Super Week itself encourages numerous interviews with athletes and affiliated sports executives, photo ops, even titillation of "new" products that might be unveiled at the viewing. "I remember, years ago, when there were only a handful of Super Bowl Parties," recounts Mitch Albom (2008, 6). "Now the parties *are* the Super Bowl. Big affairs start midweek, and the contest for the swankiest soiree is as intense as the gridiron battle."

Tailgates

> There is a kinship, caste system or social organization to tailgating. Some long-time tailgaters have parked in the same place for a decade or longer and set up their own "neighborhood watch" to make sure those time-honored places are reserved for the right fans on a Sunday. And yet, of all the things that divide us as citizens—race, ethnicity, gender, creed, age, social status—get put on hold for a while when people come together as tailgating fans.
>
> —Peter Chakerian, *The Browns Fan's Tailgating Guide* (2008, 15)

Social gatherings for food and drink before, during, and even after football games are "fan"tastic ways of making communal rituals. Probably the most popular way to celebrate, these gatherings don't necessarily need to take place at the back of a vehicle or just before the Big Event or only in parking lots, but they sure do add to the allure of partying. In fact, for Super Bowl XL1/2007, the NFL banned them, citing tailgates as security risks, but the uproar from fans and media alike was so strong that accommodations have been in place ever since.

Chakerian (2008, 19) suggests the term "tailgate" derives from the Rutgers-Princeton game of 1869 when spectators came by horse-drawn carriages and spent time prior to kick off at the "tail-end" of the horse. Yalies claim it began in New Haven in 1904, on private railcars. While the Green Bay Packers are credited with starting the practice back in 1919, today the general consensus, according to the *Bleacher Report*, is that the Kansas City Chiefs throw the best parties today, and estimates are that between 20M and 50M Americans tailgate. VIP hospitality tailgates, hosted by Pro Football Hall of Famers, ran at $1,575 for the most recent game, pre- and post- parties were ticketed at $1,299, and those with former professional athletes cost $600.

It might surprise you to know that the NFL has its own webpage dedicated to "The Art of Tailgating" <https://www.nfl.com/photos/the-art-of-tailgating-09000d5d82958263>, which is permitted in stadiums starting four hours before the game and closing about two hours after it. Between promoting coolers and cups and clothing, never mind subsidiary items, the Tailgating Industry Association (TIA) reports that the industry is worth at least $10B, and which goes up to $20B, for football alone. Drenten et al. (2009, 93) show that tailgating is "not just a party in the parking lot"; using an ethnographic approach, the sports marketing scholars found that football fans strongly identify with the practice, citing one fan's perspective:

> We spend our weeks from September through December configuring menus, showing up before 8 a.m. (at least for a 1 p.m. game), to get ready for the big game every Sunday, not just Super Sunday. The coals go on by 8:30 a.m., with eggs and sausage, and by 10 a.m. the steaks, brats, chicken, and adult beverages are being served. Man, I am already missing it! Let them tailgate!

That quotation fits with James, Breezeel, and Ross's (2011) study of tailgating that identified two primary motives among those at the University of Illinois for tailgating: to escape their normal routines and to enjoy social interaction with friends. Their results suggest the possibility of tailgating as an ancillary product for sports marketers, confirmed in Bradford and Sherry's 2015 use of the term "vestaval" in seeing tailgating as secular ritual.

Consider the number of books about the tailgating phenomenon: Joe Drozda's *The Tailgater's Handbook* (Masters Press 1996); John Madden's *Ultimate Tailgating* (Viking 1998); Robert Sloan's *Tailgating Cookbook: Recipes for the Big Game* (Chronicle 2005); Pableaux Johnson's *ESPN Gameday Gourmet: More Than 80 All-American Tailgate Recipes* (2007); Debbie Moose's *Fan Fare: A Playbook of Great Recipes for Tailgating or Watching the Game at Home* (Harvard Common Press 2007); Beth Peterson's *The Tailgate Cookbook: 75 Game-Changing Recipes for the Tastiest Tailgate Ever* (Front Table Books 2018); Ann Scheaffer's *Tailgating Done Right Cookbook: 150 Recipes for a Winning Game Day* (Fox Chapel 2019). The best scholarly one is Veri and Liberti's *Gridiron Gourmet: Gender and Food at the Football Tailgate* (2019, 4), emanating out of interest in "what happens when men dominate a cultural space—the preparation and serving of food—that is traditionally associated with women." Wanting to unpack the field, the two professors of kinesiology look at tailgating throughout media as a gendered ritual, using Guy Fieri's television show *Tailgate Warriors*, which features host city offerings from various NFL places, as a case study. "Food is a cultural product through which ethnic and racial identities are constructed, reproduced, negotiated, and realized," they write (95)—ideal accompanying thoughts to what is presented in this volume.

Party Protocol

Each individual Super Bowl has its own invitations, logo, theme song, special souvenirs, noisemaker, paper goods, favors, blogs and sign-in boards, and Party Time accessories. It is probably understood that big-screen sets are de rigueur, and television itself often plays a role in the game, often introducing new technological devices and demonstrations just for the Super Bowl (Mullen and Mazzocco 2000). It also introduces a much-anticipated array of advertisements such as these: "80,000 fans can't be wrong" about Ortega taco shells, Eckrich sausages with "Big Flavor for the Big Game," fiery sriracha for you to "get your game on," "Score big with big game appetites" (Jose Ole), Mama Lucia's meatballs as a "game changer," Frank's Red Hot as "the only winning play," Sweet Baby Ray's BBQ sauce that is "guaranteed to cover the spread," a Carvel ice cream cake as "your half-time spectacular," Pepperidge Farm buns for your "game day lineup," any number of proclaimed MVP foods, and it is always a good idea to have Tums available.

Since it is now recognized that women make up such a large section of viewers, Megan Baldwin (n.d.) offers two different possibilities for girls-only Super Bowl parties:

Play 1: The Single Girls Shuffle

- Invite all your single girlfriends over for a Gender-Bender of a Super Bowl party.
- Ask all your guests to dress (and impersonate) their favorite (or least favorite) stereotypical guy. Great examples include: The Overgrown Frat Boy, The Work-a-Holic or The Super Fan. Extra points are awarded for faux facial hair.
- No salads allowed! Make like a Skinny B++++ and girl-ify red-blooded, All-American male staples for a guilt-free menu of appetizers and finger food favorites.
- If you can't stomach a light beer, serve cans of champagne like Sofia's cute four-pack. Straws are included but remember to set out trays of chocolate cigars.
- Hold the yawns. To get the testosterone pumping while the game is on, plan a few "mock" male bonding rituals like drinking or card games.

Play 2: The Football Widow's Reverse Tackle

- Why fight over the remote? If your better half has won the coin toss and has called home-field advantage, rally a few fellow "football" widows for an away game.
- Choose a fun location. If you're in the mood for some friendly competition, stage an All-Girls Bowl-Off at a local bowling alley or take off your cleats and treat your toes to a Foot Ball at a nail salon or spa.

- For a stress-free post-game meal, find a local BYOB. Make sure to re-member to tell your guests beforehand that you plan on rallying at a restaurant. If you can't think of a good spot, ask your teammates for suggestions.
- Bring along a bottle of champagne and toast the end of the season.

Party-Throwing

A number of naysayers were wondering whether the recession would have an effect of Super Bowl XL111/2009, especially when media such as *Sports Il-lustrated* and *Playboy* canceled their annual affairs and "The annual Friday night Commissioner's Party, which has featured circus performers and wild animals, had two sand-sculpture artists instead" (Branch 2009). "The star-stud-ded parties and corporate blowouts of Super Bowl week might take a backseat to, believe it or not, the actual game," pondered Sean Gregory (2009), who pointed out how lots of participants in "America's annual weeklong baccha-nal" come for the star athletes and the celebrities. *Maxim* made like it was still delivering fantasies to its 1,400 guests, though, its editorial director, James Ka-minsky explaining, "Everyone is depressed, but everyone here is happy. That's what a good party is. It's not about saving the world. It's not about saving the whales. It's about having a good time" (cited in Branch 2009). ESPN, whose guests included Little Steven Van Zandt and Lil' Wayne, Lindsay Lohan, Vinny Testaverde, and Jared of Subway sandwich fame, was said to have thrown a "pulsating party. Sprinkled through the scene were women dancing tireless-ly, alone on pedestals. They wore referee socks, short shorts, eye black and cropped football jerseys" (cited in Branch 2009).

If you want to gamble at a Super Bowl party, BuzzFeed.com offers these silly bets:

1. Opening coin toss: Heads or Tails?
2. Will a kicker miss a field goal? Yes or No.
3. Who will throw the first interception? Three choices, "none" being one.
4. How many total points will be scored in the third quarter? Over or under 13.5.
5. Will there be a challenge flag thrown in the first half? Yes or No.
6. Will a player lose a shoe during the game? Yes or No.

7. How many songs will be performed during the Half-Time Show? Over or under 4.5.
8. How many bathroom breaks will you need from the kickoff to the final whistle? Over or under 1.5.
9. How many penalty flags will the referee throw? Over or under 2.5.
10. Which team will take the final snap of the game?

Other ideas would be rating the commercials (worst to best), voting on who will be selected MVP, giving football-related names to food, such as Patrick Mahomes meatballs, Hail Mary Bloody Mary, Gluten-free Goodell rolls, Brady bread, Joe Montana macaroni, Rob Gronkowski guacamole, Peyton Manning pizza, Troy Aikman ice cream, and such. For those more interested in partying than football-watching, you might encourage them to play *Super Bowl Charades*, with these words to get you started: (1) pre-game; (2) blindside; (3) Cheesehead; (4) referee; (5) tailgating; (6) cheerleader; (7) field goal; (8) backfield; (9) fumble; (10) helmet; (11) Buffalo Wings; (12) gridiron; (13) zigzag run; (14) ineligible receiver; (15) end zone; (16) bench player; (17) Fantasy Football; (18) pigskin; (19) quarterback; (20) touchdown.

It you are a trivia type, you can construct a quiz with questions such as *What was the coldest Super Bowl?* (A: VI: January 16, 1972 was 39°F [4°C] at kickoff in New Orleans). *Which NFL team has been in the most Super Bowl games?* (A: New England Patriots). *Who predicted Super Bowl XXXIX/2005?* (A: The Simpsons). *Which team played in a Super Bowl without scoring any touchdown?* (A: Miami Dolphins, who lost 24-3 to the Dallas Cowboys at Super Bowl V/1971).

What teams have won the most Super Bowls? (A: New England Patriots and Pittsburgh Steelers); *Who has hosted the most Super Bowl games?* (A: Miami and New Orleans). *Which team has been in four Super Bowls but never held a lead?* (A: Minnesota Vikings). *How much is the markup in host cities for Super Bowl?* (A: 101%). *Who is the record-holder for most passing yards in s Super Bowl?* (A: Tom Brady). *When did Super Bowl winners first visit the White House?* (A: 1980). *Who won every Super Bowl he played in?* (A: Joe Montana—XVI, XIX, XXXIII, XXIV). *What coach holds the record for most Super Bowl appearances?* (A: Bill Belichick). You no doubt can come up with many more.

There are a number of Super Bowl–related crosswords out there, and you can create your own version, but cards are available online for *Super Bowl Bingo*:

SUPER BOWL BINGO				
NFC Field Goal	Crying Player	Jump Over Player	Crowd Booing	Tight End Touchdown
TACO BELL Commercial	First Down	Budweiser Commercial	Receiving Touchdown	Quarterback Sack
Pass Interference	M&MS Commercial	Touchdown Dance	Holding	FEDEX Commercial
Skittles Commercial	Fumble	Fan with Face Paint	Wide Receiver Touchdown	e-Trade Commercial
Coca-Cola Commercial	Kickoff Return Touchdown	25+ Yard Run	Celebrity in Crowd	30+ Combined Points

Decorations and Events

eHow, which offers advice on fixing, building, creating, and learning about simple solutions, suggests these steps for *How to Throw a Super Bowl Party*:

- Step 1: Decorate the house in the colors of the team you're rooting for. If one of the teams playing is "your" team, put on all your parapher-nalia.
- Step 2: Invest in a few foam "bad-call bricks" to throw at the TV so your guests can express their feelings about the refs without doing damage to your house.
- Step 3: If you're going to have guests who are rooting for different teams, establish an imaginary line (or for fun, "draw" one with masking tape) down the center of the room. Decorate each side in one team's colors.
- Step 4: Order a "Super Bowl Party in a Box" that includes plates, nap-kins, cups, and a football snack bowl.
- Step 5: Pick up veggie, cheese, and cold-cut plates and a six-foot long sandwich or two from a deli and have all the food laid out on a table within sight of the TV. Don't make your guests choose between eating and watching the game.
- Step 6: Buy several six-packs of beer. Keep the beer in a cooler close by, so you don't have to run to the fridge when it's third and inches. Restock the cooler at halftime.
- Step 7: Have everyone write down who they think will win and what the final score will be before the game starts. Award a silly prize, like a big football piñata, to the person who comes the closest.

Some hosts suggest their guests dress in outfits supporting their favorite team, and you might all choose the best one(s). Kids might want to wear jerseys signifying their favorite players, and super-fans often opt for face paint. Your buffet table might be decorated with a green tablecloth divided by ten-yard lines, with posts at either end, adding football-shaped confetti. If you want to include party gifts, consider "loot bags" with NFL stickers, candles, hats, pencils, pom-poms, pennants, glow sticks, yo-yos, and/or var-ious football-related goodies. Super Bowl balloons are readily available; plus, try this suggestion for playing the game *Balloons!*, supplied by The-StarterWife (2008):

This one is easy and is played at the start and after the game is over. You pick team colors for balloons and in one set of each team colors, you place a slip of paper in each balloon…At the end of the game, each person pops a balloon. The person who pops the balloon with the slip of paper that has the total score or winning team gets the good prizes, and the losing one gets to clean the kitchen, or whatever you deem as the booby prize. You write things like "Holding, personal foul, penalty take out the garbage." Of course, the penalty is declined if it is the winning team.

"The traditional Super Bowl Party is probably the least fussy, most unpretentious party you can host all year," according to Donna Pilato (2009). "So, there is no point in holding anything back! Go all out and serve everyone's favorite high fat, finger-licking snack foods." She offers these tips for a super bash:

- Plan simple, portable foods. A buffet is your only option. Nobody wants to be sitting down at a table to eat when they'd rather be screaming at a television set or two.
- Set up as many televisions as you have available around the party area.
- Don't prepare recipes that will keep you locked in the kitchen all night. You should enjoy the party too.
- Have one room set aside without a television for partygoers who aren't interested in the game and would like a quieter place to talk.
- Likewise, set up one room with a television for serious football fans who don't want to be distracted by idle chatter.
- Plan on plenty of beverages, and don't forget the beer. With all of those beer commercials bombarding your guests, they'll be working up a strong thirst for the suds.
- If you feel compelled to decorate, think team colors, footballs, team jerseys, goal posts, and pennants. But don't knock yourself out. Most eyes will be more impressed by the clear reception on your television.
- Have lots of paper towels, napkins, and rug cleaner handy for messes created during exciting plays.
- Keep a little spare change and small bills handy for any betting pools that just might pop up over the course of the evening.

To liven things up, Mindy Kobrin (n.d.) suggests some cool musical choices:

1. *We Will Rock You/We Are the Champions*—Queen
2. *Pump It Up*—Danzel
3. *Hot in Here*—Nelly
4. *Blitzkrieg Bop*—The Ramones
5. *Celebration*—Kool and the Gang
6. *Who Let the Dogs Out*—BahaJump Around—House of Pain
8. *Whoomp!* (There It Is)—Tag Team
9. *Feelin' So Fly*—Toby McKeehan
10. *That's the Way I Like It*—KC & The Sunshine Band

Post-Game Cleanup

Once the winning team has been declared, the MVP announced, the media has reviewed for you what you have been watching for the last at least 4 hours, and it's time to face the residue of your party. Think about the 150+ professionals who have to clean up all that confetti at the stadium and somehow it should all go smoothly; after all, it's never too soon to anticipate celebrating next year's Super Bowl.

## CHAPTER 6

Post-Game Reflections on Celebrating the Super Bowl

The Super Bowl has been described as "the last chapter of a hair-raising mystery. No one would miss it."

—Pete Rozelle, former NFL Commissioner

The Super Bowl has come to permeate all corners of American life. Sermons are given in churches on Super Bowl themes. Supermarkets push Super Bowl themed food in the weeks heading into Super Sunday with special snack packs, cakes in the shape of a football, cupcakes covered with icing in the participating team colors. The beer merchants are not among the largest advertisers on the game telecast, but their displays in supermarkets establish a clear identity between their product and the Super Bowl.

—Richard Crepeau, "The Super Bowl at 50 or L." (2017, 19)

As a study in cultural criticism, this book comes full circle by again appreciating Michael Real's early insistence that sport in general, and the Super Bowl specifically, were worthy of our attention. Imagine that he had the insight, in 1975, to summarize the structural values of the Super Bowl thus: "American football is an aggressive, strictly regulated team game fought between males who use both violence and technology to win monopoly control of property for the economic gain of individuals with a nationalistic, entertainment context" (115). In his 2013 journal article "Reflections on communication and sport: On spectacle and mega-events," in *Communication & Sport*, Real reflected on that 1975 examination of it as mythic spectacle filled with "gender exclusion, racial stratification, economic return, advertiser satisfaction, heroic and antiheroic role models" in four hours of play. The Super Bowl, he concluded, "may be more spectacle than game." The excitement continues, the commodification keeps growing, and its enormous interest still predominates—despite the contingencies of COVID-19.

Things have not been going well lately for the NFL. Having weathered many storms, the league finds itself in a precarious position: Having made it through the free agency, dealing with domestic violence and accusations of sanctioned violence, athlete activism, plus the pandemic, of late it claims to be focusing on issues of social justice and health concerns related to the game. With an estimated net worth of $2.86B, money doesn't seem as much a worry as finding and maintaining star players and dealing with injuries such as those that cause brain damage. The Jon Gruden story certainly didn't help, when former ESPN analyst and coach of the Las Vegas Raiders was forced to step down in late 2021 after misogynistic and homophobic language was found in his emails relative to a racist troupe, a denunciation of a female referee, antagonism against an openly gay player, as well as nasty comments against those advocating for social equality while the national anthem was playing. "The culture runs deeper than just one head coach," Ryan Russell (2021) has shared, "Gruden's emails are not just the hateful rant of a bigot, but a written history of the vast mistreatment of marginalized voices throughout the NFL." Recognizing the NFL as a global corporate media organization, Adam Rugg (2019) has detailed how increased awareness of the medical dangers of playing the game, the emergence of luxury stadiums, and the league's philanthropic efforts all emerge as challenges. The ugly underbelly of the Super Bowl has many tentacles.

Yet, celebrations such as at Super Bowl parties provide invaluable insight into (sub)cultures of sports fans, partygoers, media industries, and the value of feminist perspectives on popular culture. "Engaging the NFL is important work for feminist scholars," Thomas P. Oates (2017) contends, "because professional football is arguably *the* key symbolic space in the contemporary United States for working through the anxieties, contradictions, and hierarchies of dominant masculinities as they struggle to adjust to a period of profound cultural, political, economic, and technological change". The mediated version of this inquiry, according to O'Donnell and Spires (2008, 2), "is a site where sporting fandom, corporate interests (large and small, but mostly large) and the state meet with varying degrees of explicit and implicit presence."

Without even discussing steroid usage, the controversy over artificial turf, the alarming number of football injuries responsible for concussions, racial oversights, ticket prices beyond the reach of regular fans, and so much more, you can at least see that football is a complex topic.

To encourage you to find out more about your favorite team(s), here are some selected references you can check out:

- *Arizona Cardinals*: Thomas K. Adamson, *The Arizona Cardinals Story* (2016); Triumph Books, *Desert Storm: Kurt Warner and the Arizona Cardinals' Unforgettable Run to the Super Bowl* (2009); Jim Whiting, *Arizona Cardinals* (2019).
- *Atlanta Falcons*: Michael E. Goodman, *The History of the Atlanta Falcons* (2005); Mark Stewart, *The Atlanta Falcons* (2009); Matt Winkeljohn, *Tales from the Atlanta Falcons Sideline* (2012).
- *Baltimore Colts*: Vince Bagli, *Sundays at 2:00 with the Baltimore Colts* (1995); George Bozeka, *The 1958 Baltimore Colts: Profiles of the NFL's First Sudden Death Champions* (2018); William Gildea, *When the Colts Belonged to Baltimore* (1994); Michael Olesker, *The Colts' Baltimore: A City and Its Love Affair in the 1950s* (2008); John F. Steadman, *From Colts to Ravens: A Behind-the-Scenes Look at Baltimore Professional Football* (2009).
- *Baltimore Ravens*: Jamison Hensley, *Flying High: Stories of the Baltimore Ravens* (2014); Tom Matte, *Tales from the Baltimore Ravens Sideline* (2017); Allan Morey, *The Baltimore Ravens Story* (2016); John Nichols, *A History of the Baltimore Ravens* (2004).
- *Buffalo Bills*: Scott Caffrey, *The Story of the Buffalo Bills* (2009); Kenneth R. Crippen, *The Original Buffalo Bills: A History of the All-America Football Conference Team, 1946–1949* (2009); Jim Gehman, *"Then Levy Said to Kelly…": The Best Buffalo Bills Stories Ever Told* (2008); Jeffrey J. Miller, *Rockin' the Rockpile: The Buffalo Bills of the AFL* (2007); Scott Pitioniak, *Buffalo Bills Football Vault: The First 50 Seasons* (2010); Randy Schultz, *Legends of the Buffalo Bills* (2003); Steve Tasker with Scott Pitoniak, *The Buffalo Bills: My Life on a Special Team* (2013); Joseph Valerio, *Second to None: The Relentless Drive and Impossible Dream of the Super Bowl Bills* (2014).
- *Carolina Panthers*: Scott Fowler, *Panthers Rising: How the Carolina Panthers Roared to the Super Bowl—And Why They'll Be Back!* (2016); Michael E. Goodman, *The Story of the Carolina Panthers* (2009); Larry Mack, *The Carolina Panthers Story* (2016); Jim Whiting, *The Story of the Carolina Panthers* (2019).
- *Chicago Bears*: *The Chicago Tribune Book of the Chicago Bears: A Decade-by-Decade History* (2015); Rich Cohen, *Monsters: The 1985 Chicago Bears and the Wild Heart of Football* (2013); Lew Freeman, *Bears by the Numbers: A Complete Team History of the Chicago Bears*

by Uniform Number (2017); Ann Marie Lipinski (Ed.), *Super Bears: The Remarkable Story of the 2006 Chicago Bears* (2007); Patrik McCaskey, *Bear with Me: A Family History of George Halas and the Chicago Bears* (2009); Kent McDill, *100 Things Bears Fans Should Know & Do before They Die* (2020); McMichael, Arvia, and Mullin, *Amazing Tales from the Chicago Bears Sideline: A Collection of the Greatest Bears Stories Ever* (2017); Allan Morey, *The Chicago Bears Story* (2016); Richard Whittingham, *We Are the Bears!:The Oral History of the Chicago Bears* (2014).

- *Cincinnati Bengals: Mary* Schmitt Boyer, *Welcome to the Jungle: Everything You Need to Know to Be a Bengals Fan* (2008); Jonathan Knight, *Paul Brown's Ghost: How the Cleveland Browns and Cincinnati Bengals Are Haunted by the Man Who Created Them* (2018); Christine Mersch, *Cincinnati Bengals History* (2006); Allan Morey, *The Cincinnati Bengals Story* (2016); Watkins and Maloney, *Classic Bengals: The 50 Greatest Games in Cincinnati Bengals History* (2018); Sam Wyche, *Tales from the Bengals Sideline* (2008).

- *Cleveland Browns*: Dave Algase, *Brown for the Count: A Compendium of Cleveland Brown Lists* (2015); Roger Gordon, *So You Think You're a Cleveland Browns Fan?* (2017); Tony Grossi, *Tales from the Cleveland Browns Sideline* (2012); Jonathan Knight, *Classic Browns: The 50 Greatest Games in Cleveland Browns History*, 2nd ed. (2015); Allan Morey, *The Cleveland Browns Story* (2016).

- *Dallas Cowboys*: Jaime Aron, *So You Think You're a Dallas Cowboys Fan?* (2016); Skip Bayless, *God's Coach: The Hymns, Hype, and Hypocrisy of Tom Landry's Cowboys* (2014); Robert W. Cohen, *The 50 Greatest Players in Dallas Cowboys History* (2017); Nick Eastman, *If These Walls Could Talk: Dallas Cowboys* (2014); John Eisenberg *Ten-Gallon War: The NFL's Cowboys, the AFL's Texans, and the Feud for Dallas's Pro Football Future* (2012); Harris and Waters, *Tales from the Dallas Cowboys Sideline* (2016); Ed Housewright, *100 Things Cowboys Fans Should Know & Do before They Die* (2015); Cody Monk, *Legends of the Dallas Cowboys: Tom Landry, Troy Aikman, Emmitt Smith, and Other Cowboys Stars* (2013); Gary Myers, *How 'bout Them Cowboys?* (2018); Joe Nick Patoski, *The Dallas Cowboys: The Outrageous History of the Biggest, Loudest, Most Hated, Best Loved Football Team in America* (2012); Jeff Pearlman, *Boys Will Be Boys: The Glory Days and Par-*

ty Nights of the Dallas Cowboys Dynasty (2009); Jim Reeves, *Dallas Cowboys: The Legends of America's Team*, 2nd ed. (2017); Jean-Jacques Taylor, *Game of My Life: Dallas Cowboys: Memorable Stories of Cowboys Football* (2012).

- *Denver Broncos*: Adrian Dater, *The Good, the Bad, and the Ugly: Heart-Pounding, Jaw-Dropping, and Gut-Wrenching Moments from Denver Broncos History* (2007); Terry Frei, *77: Denver, the Broncos, and a Coming of Age* (2009); Brian Howe, *100 Things Broncos Fans Should Know & Do before They Die* (2016); Mike Klis, *The 50 Greatest Players in Denver Broncos History* (2017); Andrew Mason, *Tales from the Denver Broncos Sideline* (2014); Allan Morey, *The Denver Broncos Story* (2016); Jim Saccomano, *Denver Broncos: The Complete Illustrated History* (2013); Matt Scheff, *Superstars of the Denver Broncos* (2013).

- *Green Bay Packers*: Michael Bauman, *Ron Wolf and the Green Bay Packers: Mike Holmgren, Brett Favre, Reggie White, and the Pack's Return to Glory in the 1990s* (2019); Mark Beech, *The People's Team: An Illustrated History of the Green Bay Packers* (2019); Bob Berghaus, *The First America's Team: The 1962 Green Bay Packers* (2011); Butler and Reischel, *Packers Pride: Green Bay Greats Share Their Favorite Memories* (2013); Chuck Carlson, *Ice Bowl '67: The Packers, the Cowboys, and the Game That Changed the NFL* (2017); Judy DuCharme, *The Cheesehead Devotional* (2012); Don Gulbrandsen, *Green Bay Packers: The Complete Illustrated History* (2011); Larrivee and Reischel, *If These Walls Could Talk: Green Bay Packers* (2016); Vince Lombardi, *Run to Daylight!: A Week in the NFL with the Green Bay Packers* (2010); David Marannis, *When Pride Still Mattered: A Life of Vince Lombardi* (1999); Allan Morey, *The Green Bay Packers Story* (2016); Larry D. Names, *The History of the Green Bay Packers: The Shameful Years* (2018); Olson and Wilde, *The Big 50: Green Bay Packers: The Men and Moments That Made the Green Bay Packers* (2019); William Povletich, *Green Bay Packers: Trials, Triumphs, and Tradition* (2012); Rob Reischel, *Leaders of the Pack: Starr, Favre, Rodgers and Why Green Bay's Quarterback Trio Is the Best in NFL History* (2015); Joe Zagorski, *The Year the Packers Came Back: Green Bay's 1972 Resurgence* (2019).

- *Indianapolis Colts*: Mike Chappell, *Game of My Life: Indianapolis Colts: Memorable Stories of Colts Football* (2016); Nate Dunlevy, *Blue Blood:*

The History of the Indianapolis Colts (2017); Lew Freedman, *Indianapolis Colts: The Complete Illustrated History* (2013); Tyler Omoth, *The Story of the Indianapolis Colts* (2009).

- *Kansas City Chiefs*: Bill Althaus, *The Good, the Bad, and the Ugly: Heart-Pounding, Jaw-Dropping, and Gut-Wrenching Moments in Kansas City Chiefs History* (2007); Matt Derrick, *At Last! The Kansas City Chief's Unforgettable 2019 Championship Season* (2020); Jeff Deters, *Kansas City Chiefs Legends: The Greatest Coaches, Players and Front Office Execs in Chiefs History* (2019); Bob Gretz, *Tales from the Kansas City Chiefs Sideline: A Collection of the Greatest Chiefs Stories Ever Told* (2015); Allan Morey, *The Kansas City Chiefs Story* (2016); Mark Stallard, *Kansas City Chiefs Encyclopedia,* 3rd ed. (2013).
- *Los Angeles Raiders*: Joseph Hession, *Raiders: Collector's Edition* (1991); Pat Ryan, *The Los Angeles Raiders* (1991).
- *Los Angeles Rams*: Jim Hock, *Hollywood's Team: The Story of the 1950s Los Angeles Rams and Pro Football's Golden Age* (2016); Allan Morey, *The Los Angeles Rams Story* (2016); Bob Oates, *The Los Angeles Rams: The Inside Story of the Coaches, Owners, and Players Who Built the World's Most Colorful Football Team* (1955); Jim Whiting, Jim (2019). *The Story of the Los Angeles Rams* (2019).
- *Miami Dolphins*: Andy Cohen, *Fins at 50: Celebrating a Half Century of Miami Dolphins Football* (2016); Griese and Hyde, *Perfection: The Inside Story of the 1972 Miami Dolphins' Perfect Season* (2012); Adam Schmalzbauer, *The History of the Miami Dolphins* (2004); Sun-Sentinel, *The Dolphins at 50: Legends and Memories from South Florida's Most Celebrated Team* (2015); Yepremian and Clayton, *Tales from the Miami Dolphins Sideline* (2012).
- *Minnesota Vikings*: Bill Ballew, *Tough Enough to Be Vikings: Minnesota's Purple Pride* (1999); Jim Bruton, *Vikings 50: All-Time Greatest Players in Franchise History* (2012); Mark Craig, *100 Things Vikings Fans Should Know and Do before They Die* (2012); Marty Gitlin, *Minnesota Vikings* (2010); Holien and Belatti, *Purple People: The Crazy Culture and Customs of Minnesota Vikings Fans, the Best Fans in the NFL* (2006); Armand Peterson, *The Vikings Reader* (2009); Tiger Vidmar, *Bleeding' Purple: The History of the Minnesota Vikings1961-Present* (2016); Bill Williamson, *Tales from the Minnesota Vikings Sideline: A Collection of the Greatest Viking Stories Ever Told* (2012).

- *New England Patriots*: Troy Brown, *Patriot Pride: My Life in the New England Dynasty* (2015); Mike Felger, *Tales from the New England Patriots Sideline* (2017); Vin Femia, *Patriot Pride: The 50 Year Rise of the New England Patriots as Seen through a Fan's Eyes* (2010); Sean Glennon, Sean *Tom Brady vs. the NFL: The Case for Football's Greatest Quarterback* (2012); Rob Gronkowki, Rob *It's Good to Be Gronk* (2015); David Halberstam, *Education of a Coach: Belichick* (2005); Michael Holley, *Belichick and Brady: Two Men, the Patriots, and How They Revolutionized Football* (2016); Pepper Johnson, *Won for All: The Inside Story of the New England Patriots' Improbable Run to the Super Bowl* (2003); Brian Kelly, *Great Moments in New England Patriots Football* (2018); James K. Lavin, *Management Secrets of the New England Patriots: From "Patsies" to 3-Time Super Bowl Champs* (2005); Leadership Case Studies *Strategy Concepts of Bill Belichick: A Leadership Case Study of the New England Patriots Head Coach* (2015); Ian O'Connor, *Belichick: The Making of the Greatest Football Coach of All Time* (2018); Charles P. Pierce, *Moving the Chains: Tom Brady and the Pursuit of Everything* (2008) and *The Blueprint: How the New England Patriots Beat the System to Create the Last Great NFL Superpower* (2008); Christopher Price, *New England Patriots: The Complete Illustrated History* (2013) and *Drive for Five: The Remarkable Run of the 2016 Patriots* (2017); Michael Sandler, Michael (2007). *Tom Brady and the New England Patriots: Super Bowl XXXVIII* (2007); Sherman and Wedge, *12: The Inside Story of Tom Brady's Fight for Redemption* (2018); Bob Socci, *New England Patriots: The Greatest Ever* (2017); Stout and Johnson, *The Pats: An Illustrated History of the New England Patriots* (2018); Jerry Thornton, *From Darkness to Dynasty: The First 40 Years of the New England Patriots* (2018); Jerry Thornton, *Five Rings: The Super Bowl History of the New England Patriots (So Far)* (2018); Zolak and Howe, *If These Walls Could Talk: New England Patriots: Stories from the New England Patriots Sideline, Locker Room, and Press Box* (2018).
- *New Orleans Saints*: Drew Brees, *Coming Back Stronger: Unleashing the Hidden Power of Adversity* (2010); Jeff Duncan, Jeff, *Tales from the New Orleans Saints Sideline: A Collection of the Greatest Saints Stories Ever Told* (2012); Reid Gilbert, *Of Bread and Circuses: The Story of Bountygate and the 2012 New Orleans Saints* (2013); Larry Mack, *The*

New Orleans Saints Story (2016); Sean Payton, *Home Team: Coaching the Saints and New Orleans Back to Life* (2010); Michael Sandler, *Drew Brees and the New Orleans Saints: Super Bowl XL1V* (2011); Casey Schreiber, *Saints in the Broken City: Football, Fandom and Urban Renewal in Post-Katrina New Orleans* (2016); Christian Serpas, *The New Orleans Saints: 25 Years of Heroic Effort* (1992); Creg Stephenson, *Marching in: The World Champion New Orleans Saints* (2010).

- *New York Giants*: Jerry Barca, *Big Blue Wrecking Crew: Smashmouth Football, a Little Bit of Crazy, and the '86 Super Bowl Champion New York Giants* (2017); Bendetson and Marshall, *When the Cheering Stops: Bill Parcells, the 1990 New York Giants, and the Price of Greatness* (2010); Ira Berkow, *Giants among Men: Y.A., L.T., the Big Tuna, and Other New York Giants Stories* (2015); Saulie Blumberg, *New York Giants* (2016); Mark Bowden, *The Best Game Ever: Giants vs Colts, 1958, and the Birth of the Modern NFL* (2009); Jack Cavanaugh, *Giants among Men: How Robustelli, Huff, Gifford, and the Giants Made New York a Football Town and Changed the NFL* (2017); Bill Chastain, *100 Things Giants Fans Should Know & Do before They Die* (2011); Robert W. Cohen, *The 50 Greatest Players in New York Giants Football History* (2018); Tom Coughlin, *A Team to Believe in: Our Journey to the Super Bowl Championship* (2008); Carlo DeVito, *Wellington: The Maras, the Giants, and the City of New York* (2006) and *Parcells: A Biography* (2011); Roger Director, *I Dream in Blue: Life, Death, and the New York Giants* (2009); Lew Freedman, *New York Giants: The Complete Illustrated History* (2009).

- Frank Gifford, *The Glory Game: How the 1958 NFL Championship Changed Football Forever* (2008); Michael E. Goodman, *The Story of the New York Giants* (2009).

- Michael E. Keneski, *The Super Season: The Story of the 2012 Super Bowl Champion New York Giants* (2012); John Maxymuk, *The 50 Greatest Plays in New York Giants Football History* (2008); *Game Changers: New York Giants: The Greatest Plays in New York Giants History* (2010); and the *New York Post* article, "Deja Blue: The New York Giants' 2011 Championship Season" (2012); Ernie Palladino (2013). *If These Walls Could Talk: Stories from the New York Giants' Sidelines, Locker Room, and Press Box* (2013); Ken Palmer, *Game of My Life: New York Giants: Memorable Stories of Giants Football* (2012); Bill Parcells, *Parcells: A*

Football Life (2014); Arthur Pincus, *New York Giants Pride: The Amazing Story of the New York Giants Road to Victory in Super Bowl XL11* (2008); Tom Rock, *Miracle Moments in New York Giants Football History* (2019).

- Matt Scheff, *Superstars of the New York Giants* (2013); Paul Schwartz, *Tales from the New York Giants Sideline: A Collection of the Greatest Giants Stories Ever Told* (2017).

- Pat Summerall, *Giants: What I Learned about Life from Vince Lombardi and Tom Landry* (2010); Richard Whittingham, *Illustrated History of the New York Giants: A Visual Celebration of Football's Beloved Franchise* (2005); Whittingham and Buscema (2014). *We Are the Giants: The Oral History of the New York Giants* (2014); Steve Zipay, *Then Bavaro Said to Simms: The Best New York Giants Stories Ever Told* (2011).

- *New York Jets*: Dave Anderson, *Countdown to Super Bowl: How the 1968–69 New York Jets Delivered on Joe Namath's Guarantee to Win It All* (2018); Mark Cannizzaro, *Tales from the New York Jets Sideline: A Collection of the Greatest Jets Stories Ever Told* (2016); Gerald Eskenazi, *Gang Green: An Irreverent Look Behind the Scenes at 38 (Well, 37) Seasons of New York Jets Football Futility* (2010); Bert Flieger, *The Wonder Year: The Championships of the New York Jets, Mets, and Knicks Were Only Part of the Story in 1969* (2017); Jeff Freier, *Jets Underground: Wahoo, Joe Willie, and the Swingin' Swaggerin' World of Gang Green* (2011); Michael E. Goodman, *The Story of the New York Jets* (2009); Ed Gruver, *From Baltimore to Broadway: Joe, the Jets, and the Super Bowl III Guarantee (*2009);Mark Kriegel, *Namath: A Biography* (2005); Bo Lederer, *Beyond Broadway Joe: The Super Bowl Team That Changed Football* (2018); Joe Namath, *I Can't Wait "til Tomorrow…" Cause I Get Better Looking Every Day* (1969) and *All the Way: My Life in Four Quarter*s (2019); Greg Prato, *Sack Exchange: The Definitive Oral History of the 1980s New York Jets* (2011); William J. Ryczek, *Crash of the Titans: The Early Years of the New York Jets and the AFL* (2009); Steve Serby, *No Substitute for Sundays: Brett Favre and His Year in the Huddle with the New York Jets* (2009); Brett Topel, *When Shea Was Home: The Story of the 1975 Mets, Yankees, Giants, and Jets* (2016).

- *Oakland Raiders*: Chandler and Fox, *Violent Sundays: Oakland Raiders* (1984); Glenn Dickey, *Just Win, Baby: Al Davis and His Raiders* (1991); Tom Flores, *Tales from the Oakland Raiders Sideline (*2012);

Paul Gutierrez, *100 Things Raiders Fans Should Know & Do before They Die* (2014); John Lombardo, *Raiders Forever: Stars of the NFL's Most Colorful Team Recall Their Glory Days* (2000); Allan Morey, *The Oakland Raiders Story* (2016); Peter Richmond, *Badasses: The Legend of Snake, Foo, Dr. Death, and John Madden's Oakland Raiders* (2011); Siani and Clark, *Cheating Is Encouraged: A Hard-Nosed History of the 1970s Raiders* (2017).

- *Philadelphia Eagles*: Sam O. Barlow, *Twas the Night before Eagles: My Super Bowl Dream Comes True* (2018); Zach Berman, *Underdogs: The Philadelphia Eagles' Emotional Road to Super Bowl Victory* (2010); Chuck Carlson, *100 Things Eagles Fans Should Know & Do before They Die* (2011); Skip Clayton, *So You Think You're a Philadelphia Eagles Fan?? Stars, Stats, Records and Memories for True Diehards* (2017); Robert W. Cohen, *The 50 Greatest Players in Philadelphia Eagles History* (2019); Turron Davenport, *Carson Wentz: Soaring with the Eagles* (2018); Ray Didinger, *The Eagles Encyclopedia: Champions Edition* (2018); *Eagles Fly: The Underdog Philadelphia Eagles' Historic 201 Championship Season* (2018); Mark Eckel, *Big 50: Philadelphia Eagles: The Men and the Moments That Made the Philadelphia Eagles* (2016); Gordon Forbes, *Tales from the Philadelphia Eagles Sidelines: A Collection of the Greatest Eagles Stories Ever Told* (2017); Reuben and Eckel, *Game Changers: Philadelphia Eagles: The 50 Greatest Plays in Philadelphia Eagles Football History* (2009); Frank and Eckel, *The Philadelphia Eagles Playbook: Inside the Huddle for the Greatest Plays in Eagles History* (2015); Bo Gordon, *The 1960 Philadelphia Eagles: The Team That They Said Had Nothing but a Championship* (2001) and *Game of My Life: Philadelphia Eagles: Memorable Stories of Eagles Football* (2018); KCI Sports Publishing, *Flying High: Celebrating a World Championship for the Philadelphia Eagles* (2018); Brian Kelly, *The Great Moments in Philadelphia Eagles Football* (2019); Rob Maaddi, *Birds of Pray: The Story of the Philadelphia Eagles' Faith, Brotherhood, and Super Bowl Victory* (2018); Sal Paolantonio, *Philly Special: The Inside Story of How the Philadelphia Eagles Won Their First Super Bowl Championship* (2018); Fran Zimniuch, *Eagles: Where Have You Gone?* (2004).
- *Pittsburgh Steelers*: Roy Blount, *About Three Bricks Shy of a Load: A Highly Irregular Lowdown on a Year the Pittsburgh Steelers Were Super*

but Missed the Bowl (2013); Terry Bradshaw, *Keep It Simple* (2002); Scott Brown, *Pittsburgh Steelers Fans' Bucket List* (2016); Bill Chastain, *Steel Dynasty: The Team That Changed the NFL* (2005); Robert W. Cohen, *The 50 Greatest Players in Pittsburgh Steelers History* (2019); David Finoli, *Classic Steelers: The 50 Greatest Games in Pittsburgh Steelers History* (2014); Matt Fulks, *The Good, the Bad & the Ugly: Heart-Pounding, Jaw-Dropping, and Gut-Wrenching Moments from Pittsburgh Steelers History* (2008); Dale Grdnic, *Pittsburgh Steelers Glory Days* (2013); Gruver and Campbell, *Hell with the Lid Off: Inside the Fierce Rivalry between the 1970s Oakland Raiders and Pittsburgh Steelers* (2019); Steve Hickoff, *The 50 Greatest Plays in Pittsburgh Steelers Football History* (2008) and *The Pittsburgh Steelers Playbook: Inside the Huddle for the Greatest Plays in Steelers History* (2015); Ilkin and Williams, *Forged in Steel: The Seven Time-Tested Leadership Principles Practiced by the Pittsburgh Steelers* (2013); Tunch Ilkin, *In the Locker Room: Tales of the Pittsburgh Steelers from the Playing Field to the Broadcast Booth* (2018); Brian Kelly, *Great Coaches in Pittsburgh Steelers Football* (2018); Matt Loede, *100 Things Steelers Fans Should Know & Do before They Die* (2013) and *Game of My Life: Pittsburgh Steelers: Memorable Stories of Steelers Football* (2015); John McFarland (Ed.), *Facing the Pittsburgh Steelers: Players Recall the Glory Years of the Black and Gold* (2016); Abby Mendelson, *The Pittsburgh Steelers: The Official Team History* (1996) and *The Steelers Experience: A Year-by-Year Chronicle of the Pittsburgh Steelers* (2014); Miller and Allen, *Always a Home Game: Our Journey through Steelers County in 140 Days* (2014); Millman and Coyne, *The Ones Who Hit the Hardest: The Steelers, the Cowboys, the '70s, and the Fight for America's Soul* (2010); Allan Morey, *The Pittsburgh Steelers Story* (2016); *Pittsburgh Post-Gazette, Super Six: The Steelers Record Setting Super Bowl Season* (2009); Gary Pomerantz, *Their Life's Work: The Brotherhood of the 1970s Pittsburgh Steelers, Then and Now* (2013); Dan Rooney, *My 75 Years with the Pittsburgh Steelers and the NFL* (2008); Michael Sandler, *Hines Ward and the Pittsburgh Steelers: Super Bowl XL* (2007), *Santonio Holmes and the Pittsburgh Steelers: Super Bowl XXL111* (2007), *Peyton Manning and the Indianapolis Colts: Super Bowl XL1* (2007), and *Ben Roethlisberger* (2009); Jim Wexell, *Pittsburgh Steelers: Men of Steel* (2011) and *Tales from Behind the Steel Curtain: The Best Stories of the '79 Steelers* (2012); Jason Zemcik, *Black and Gold Dynasty: The Championship History of the Pittsburgh Steelers* (2017).

- *San Diego Chargers*: Sid Brooks, *Tales from the San Diego Chargers Sideline* (2014); Allan Morey, *The San Diego Chargers Story* (2016); Tyler Omoth, *The Story of the San Diego Chargers* (2009); Jay Paris, *Game of My Life: San Diego Chargers: Memorable Stories of Chargers Football* (2016); Dave Steidel, *The Uncrowned Champs: How the 1963 San Diego Chargers Would Have Won the Super Bowl* (2015); Todd Tobias, *Charging through the AFL: Los Angeles and San Diego Chargers' Football in the 1960s* (2004).

- *San Francisco 49ers*: Daniel Brown, *100 Things 49ers Fans Should Know and Do before They Die* (2013); Roger Craig, *Tales from the San Francisco 49ers Sideline: A Collection of the Greatest 49ers Stories Ever Told* (2012); Glenn Dickey, *The San Francisco 49ers: The First 50 Years* (1995); Gordon Forbes, *When the 49ers Were Kings: How Bill Walsh and Ed DeBartola Jr. Built a Football Dynasty in San Francisco* (2018); Dennis Georgatos, *Game of My Life: San Francisco 49ers: Memorable Stories of 49ers Football* (2013); Martin Jacobs, *San Francisco 49ers Legends: The Golden Age of Pro Football* (2016); Matt Maiocco, *San Francisco 49ers: The Complete Illustrated History* (2013); Brian Murphy, *San Francisco 49ers: From Kezar to Levi's Stadium* (2014); Dave Newhouse, *The Million Dollar Backfield: The San Francisco 49ers in the 1950s* (2000) and *Founding 49ers: The Dark Days before the Dynasty* (2015); Dennis Pottenger, *Great Expectations: The San Francisco 49ers and the Quest for the "Three-Peat"* (1991); Jerry Rice, *Go Long! My Journey Beyond the Game and the Fame* (2007) and *America's Game: The NFL at 100* (2019); Michael Sandler, *Joe Montano and the San Francisco 49ers: Super Bowl XXIV* (2009); Steve Silverman, *"Then Steve Said to Jerry…": The Best San Francisco 49ers Stories Ever Told* (2008); Steven Travers, *The Good, the Bad, and the Ugly: Heart-Pounding, Jaw-Dropping, and Gut-Wrenching Moments from San Francisco 49ers History* (2009); Chris Willis, *A Nearly Perfect Season: The Inside Story of the 1984 San Francisco 49ers* (2011); Dave Zirin, *The Kaepernick Effect: Taking a Knee, Changing the World* (2012).

- *Seattle Seahawks*: Paul Allen, *World Champion Seattle Seahawks: We Are 12* (2014); Chris Cluff, *The Good, the Bad, and the Ugly: Seattle Seahawks: Heart-Pounding, Jaw-Dropping, and Gut-Wrenching Moments from Seattle Seahawks History* (2007); Derrick Coleman, *No Excuses: Growing Up Deaf and Achieving My Super Bowl Dream*s (2015); Brian Lester, *Seattle Seahawks* (2010); Fred Moody, *Fighting Chance: An NFL Season with the Seattle Seahawks* (1989); Allan Morey, *Superstars of the Seattle Seahawks* (2018); John Morgan, *100 Things Seahawks Fans Should Know and Do before They Die* (2010); Moyer and Wyman, *"Then Zorn Said to Largent…": The Best Seattle Seahawks Stories Ever Told* (2008); Steve Raible, *Tales from the Seattle Seahawks Sideline* (2012); Mark Tye Turner, *Notes from a 12 Man: A Truly Biased History of the Seattle Seahawks* (2010) and *Seattle Seahawks Super Season: Notes from a 12 on the Best Season in Seahawks History* (2014); Dave Wyman, *If These Walls Could Talk: Stories from the Seattle Seahawks Sideline, Locker Room, and Press Box* (2019).

- *St. Louis Rams*: Lonnie Bell, *The History of the St. Louis Rams* (2004); Aaron Frisch, *The Story of the St. Louis Rams* (2013); Michael Sandler, *Kurt Warner and the St. Louis Rams: Super Bowl XXXIV* (2007); Mark Stewart, *The St. Louis Rams* (2012).

- *Tampa Bay Buccaneers*: Dennis M. Crawford, *Hugh Culverhouse and the Tampa Bay Buccaneers: How a Skinflint Genius with a Losing Team Made the Modern NFL* (2011); Max Hater, *Reasons to Be a Buccaneers Fan: An Intelligent Guide* (2017); Michael Sandler, *Dexter Jackson and the Tampa Bay Buccaneers: Super Bowl XXXIII* (2008); Jason Vuic, *The Yucks: Two Years in Tampa with the Losingest Team in NFL History* (2016).

- *Washington Redskins*: Alan Beall, *Braves on the Warpath: The 50 Greatest Games in the History of the Washington Redskins* (1988); Thomas Boswell, *Redskins: A History of Washington's Team* (1997); Richard C. King, *Redskins: Insult and Brand* (2016); Keith Landry, *Raising the Teepee: Washington Redskins Drafts, Trades, Drama 1960–1972* (2015); Adam Lazarus, *Hail to the Redskins: Gibbs, the Diesel, the Hogs, and the Glory Days of D.C.'s Football Dynasty* (2015); Thom Loverro, *Hail Victory: An Oral History of the Washington Redskins* (2008); Andrew O'Toole, *Fight for Old D.C.: George Preston Marshall, the Integration of the Washington Redskins, and the Rise of a New NFL* (2016); Michael Richman, *The Redskins Encyclopedia* (2009); Thomas G. Smith, *Showdown: JFK and the Integration of the Washington Redskins* (2011); Richard Whittingham, *Hail Redskins: A Celebration of the Greatest Players,*

Teams, and Coaches (2004). Also significant are Ray Walker's *The Ul-timate Washington Football Team Trivia Book* and Conroy Charles' *The Washington Football Team Encyclopedia* of 2021.

"As a sporting event, the Super Bowl represents the season's culmination of a ma-jor American game," Joseph L. Price (2001, 140) has commented. "As a popular spectacle, it encourages endorsement by politicians and incorporates elements of nationalism. And as a cultural festival, it commands vast allegiance while drama-tizing and reinforcing the religious myths of national innocence and apotheosis."

Super Sunday has grown exponentially in its more than four decades of offer-ing the fun of competition to exemplifying the penultimate Big Business model not only for how to throw football passes but also for how to host a party. The quintessential sporting event has become the quintessential party one, too. And, when all is said and done, we can only hope that you enjoy yourself as host or guest at a Super Bowl party and that you and your designated favorite team score! Here are hosts for future games:

2021 Tampa, FL
2022 Los Angeles Stadium at Hollywood Park, Inglewood, CA
2023 University of Phoenix Stadium, Glendale, AZ
2024 Mercedes-Benz Superdome, New Orleans, LA

The current NFL season turns out to be its longest, lasting eighteen weeks, each team playing seventeen games and having a bye week. Then come the playoffs—extended, with seven entrants from each sixteen-team conference. The scheduled date for Super Bowl LVI/2022 is the latest ever: February 13th, at SoFi Stadium, Los Angeles. Hopefully you will be using and quoting this book that day!

"The Super Bowl symbolizes the fundamental sports paradox for me," Stan-ley D. Eitzen (2016) has figured out. "It is both magical and materialistic, uni-fying and divisive, inclusive and exclusionary, expansive and exploitative." As we move toward technological "advances" for football in terms of training, equipment, security, and analytics, it seems safe to predict that the Super Bowl will be with us for the long haul. Clearly, it is much more than just a sporting event; instead, it is a sociocultural phenomenon with enormous national and global audiences, deep economic impact and implications, and racial, medical, media, even celebratory subsets. That becomes worth examining in terms of gendered rhetoric. Hopefully this book helps answer some questions that Michael Real's influential essay posited back in 1975:

- Why is the Super Bowl the most lucrative annual spectacle on American media?
- When were electronic media wedded with spectator sports?
- How do mass-mediated cultural events resemble ancient mythic rituals?
- How does the Super Bowl fulfill contemporary mythic-ritual functions?
- What is the essential internal structure of North American football, and how does it parallel structures in American society?
- Are there sexism, racism, and authoritarianism in the Super Bowl?
- How does Super Bowl football compare with other sports in the West and with sports in contrasting non-Western cultures?
- How can the Super Bowl be both a propaganda vehicle serving a power structure and an enjoyable choice of viewers? (92)

People have asked me, why the Super Bowl? And my instant response to it is my abiding interest in mega-events, but clearly it is more than that. It reminds me of a question on my undergraduate comprehensive exams for American Studies, when we were asked to choose something for a time capsule. What could be more appropriate than this annual day-off for friendship and football (and food!) that includes so many American themes, such as gigantism, patriotism, militarism, consumerism, escapism, heroism, hedonism, individualism, and the ultimate irony in that we, the audience, are the product? When, relative to Super Bowl LIV/2020, *New York Times* asked three of its culture critics why they even watch ("It's flawed. It's Ugly. It's beautiful"—January 31, 2020), Austin Considine wrote: "The Super Bowl isn't just a game. It's the half-time show; it's the ads; it's the chips and guac. It is sport but also music, dance, costumes, TV production and stage design—a pop-culture event greater than the sum of its parts." Think of it this way: Super Sunday is the biggest day for consumption—a festival of consumerism, if you will, of both food and football. It is perhaps no better a barometer of our twin obsessions of food and football. And—you now know, so much more.

As you circle your calendars for future Super Bowls—**Super Bowl LVII:** February 12, 2023, State Farm Stadium, Glendale, Arizona; **Super Bowl LVIII:** 2024, Allegiant Stadium, Las Vegas, Nevada; and Super Bowl LIX: 2025, Caesars Superdome, New Orleans, Louisiana, hopefully this book will encourage you to be a "critical viewer/celebrator."

REFERENCES

Ackley, Brian, David Levinson, and Gerald Gems. 2019. "The Super Bowl: An American Institution." In *Touchdown: An American Obsession Goes Global*, edited by Gerald R. Gems and Gertrud Pfister, 55–57. Great Barrington, MA: Berkshire Publishing.

Adamson, Melitta Weiss, and Francine Segan. 2008. *Entertaining from Ancient Rome to the Super Bowl*. Westport, CT: Greenwood Press.

Albom, Mitch. 2008. "Five Things You Might Not Know about the Super Bowl." *Parade*, February 3, 2008:6–7.

Anastasio, Dina. 2019. *What Is the Super Bowl?* New York: Penguin Workshop.

Anthony, Jason. 2012. "The Holy Game: Gold Plays on Super Bowl Sunday." *Boston Review*, February 3, 2012.

Aron, James. 2011. *Breakthrough 'Boys: The Story of the 1971 Super Bowl Champion Dallas Cowboys*. Minneapolis, MN: MVP Books.

Axelrad, Jacob. 2014. "Roger Goodell Solution to NFL Domestic Violence: 'Everything is on the table.'" *The Christian Science Monitor*, September 19.

Axson, Scooby. 2017. "'Concussion' Doctor: Letting Kids Play Football is 'Definition of Child Abuse.'" *Sports Illustrated*, August 8.

Azzi, Alex. 2021. "Women at the Super Bowl: A Brief History of Football's Pioneering Women." *NBC Sports*, February 9, 2021.

Babiak, Kathy, and Richard Wolfe. 2006. "More Than Just a Game? Corporate Social Responsibility and Super Bowl XL." *Sport Marketing Quarterly* 15 (4): 214–222.

Baldwin, Megan. n.d. "Tips for Girls only Super Bowl Party." http://www.celebrations.com/content/Tips-For-Girls-Only-Super-Bowl-Party.

Bauer, Ethan. 2020. "What Makes the Super Bowl So American?" *Deseret News*, February 1, 2020.

Belson, Ken. 2020. "NFL Relaxes Restrictions on Marijuana Use as Part of New Labor Deal." *New York Times*, April 13, 2020: D1, 4.

Belson, Ken. 2021. "At the Super Bowl, the NFL's Social Message Is Muddled." *New York Times*, February 8, 2021.

Belson, Ken. 2022. "Two Punishing Hits in Five Days Renew Protocol Criticisms." *New York Times*, October 1, 2022.

Bendetson, William, and Leonard Marshall. 2010. *When the Cheering Stops: Bill Parcells, the 1990 New York Giants, and the Price of Greatness*. Chicago: Triumph Books.

Bennett, Lisa. 2003. "Madison Avenue Meets Super Bowl: Witless Ads Gave Us Sex, Violence and Yes, Vomit." *Media Report to Women* 31 (1): 1–3.

Bennett, Michael and Dave Zirin. 2018. *Things that Make White People Uncomfortable*. Chicago: Haymarket Books.

Berghaus, Bob. 2008. *Black and Blue: A Smash-Mouth History of the NFL's Roughest Division*. New York: Clerisy Press.

Berman, Jillian. 2013. "Americans Eat 1,083,333 Football Fields Worth of Wings on Super Bowl Sunday and Other Fun Facts." *Huffington Post*, February 2, 2013.

Berman, Lazar. 2021. "The Insider's Guide to Super Bowl LV's Jewish Stories and Subplots." *Times of Israel*, February 8, 2021.

Berns, Nancy. 2001. "Degendering the Problem and Gendering the Blame: Political Discourse on Women and Violence." *Gender & Society* 15 (2): 262–281.

Beschloss, Michael. 2015. "AFL vs NFL: The time before the Bowl was Super." *The Bulletin*, January 31.

Bianchi, Eugene. 1974. "The Super Bowl Culture of Male Violence." *Christian Century*, September 18, 1974:842–845.

Billick, Brian, and Michael MacCambridge. 2009. *More Than a Game: The Glorious Present and Uncertain Future of the NFL*. New York: Scribner.

Birle, Pete. 2015. *Broadway Joe*. La Jolla, CA: Scobre Educational.

Bishop, Greg. 2007. "Super Bowl: The Holiest Day of the Season." *Seattle Times*, February 3, 2007.

Bissinger, H G ("Buzz"). 1991. *Friday Night Lights: A Town, a Team, and a Dream*. New York: HarperCollins.

Blackburn, Pete. 2020. "Super Bowl Parties in Miami: Times and Dates, Celebrity Guests and What to Know about the Best Events." *CBS Sports.com*, February 1, 2020.

Blanco, Abigail R. Hall. 2021. "Manufacturing Militarism: US Government Propaganda in the War on Terror." *Independent Institute*, February 8, 2021.

Bohnert, Suzy Beamer. 2007. *Game-Day Goddess: Learning Football's Lingo*. Arlington, VA: B&B Publishing.

Bowden, Mark. 2009. *The Best Game Ever: Giants vs Colts, 1958, and the Birth of the Modern NFL*. New York: Grove Press.

Bowers, David. 2014. *The Ultimate Sports Fans' Cookbook: Festive Recipes for Inside the Home and Outside the Stadium*. New York: Skyhorse.

Bradford, Tonya Williams and John F. Sherry, Jr. 2015. "Domesticating Public Space Through Ritual: Tailgating as Vestaval." *Journal of Consumer Research* 42: 130-151

Brady, James. 2009. "In Step with Al Michaels." *Parade*, February 1, 2009:14.

Branch, John. 2009. "Despite the Recession, It's Still Party Time." *New York Times*, February 1, 2009: SP7.

Branch, Taylor. 2011. "The Shame of College Sports." *Atlantic*, October 10, 2011.

Brassil, Gillian R., and Kevin Draper. 2021. "NFL 'Firsts' Look Forward to Having More Company." *New York Times*, February 4, 2021.

Breech, John. 2016. "Fans at Super Bowl 50 Spend Nearly $11 Million, Bought 8K Glasses of Wine." *CBS Sports.com*, February 11, 2016.

Brown, Francis. 2013. *Handicapping the NFL: Win Consistently Year After Year*. CreateSpace Independent Publishing Platform.

Brown, Maleaha L. 2016. "When Pros Become Cons: Ending the NFL's History of Domestic Violence Leniency." *Family Law Quarterly* 50 (1): 193–212.

Bruinius, Harry. 2019. "'Be a Man': What Does That Mean in Modern America?" *Christian Science Monitor*, February 1, 2019.

Buchwald, Elizabeth. 2020. "Super Bowl 2020 Tickets Now Cost an Average of $10,000." *Market Watch*, February 2, 2020.

Butterworth, Michael L. 2008. "Fox Sports, Super Bowl XL11, and the Affirmation of American Civil Religion." *Journal of Sport & Social Issues* 32:318–323.

Callahan, Rick. 2012. "Keeping Warm at Super Bowl." *Republican*, January 30, 2012.

Capello, Gregoary. 2012. *The Guide to NFL Investing: The Football Betting System of an Investment Professional*. CreateSpace Independent Publishing Platform.

Carlson, Chuck. 2009. *Green Bay Packers: Yesterday & Today*. Lincolnwood, IL: West Side Publishing.

Carneiro, Robert L. 2006. *Diary of a Football Handicapper*. Indiana: AuthorHouse.

Caron, Sandra L., and J. Michael Hodgson. 2011. *Tackling Football: A Woman's Guide to Understanding the College Game*. Orono, ME: Maine College Press.

Chakerian, Peter. 2008. *The Browns Fan's Tailgating Guide*. Cleveland, OH: Gray.

Christopher, Matt. 2006. *The Super Bowl: Legendary Sports Events*. New York: Little, Brown Books for Young Readers.

Coenen, Craig R. 2005. *From Sandlots to the Super Bowl: The National Football League, 1920–1967*. Knoxville: University of Tennessee Press.

Coleman, Candy. 1980. *Pigskin Picnics*. Mt. Pocono, Pennsylvania: CC Enterprises

Coleman, Derrick with Marcus Brotherton. 2015. *No Excuses: Growing Up Deaf and Achieving my Super Bowl Dreams*. New York: Gallery/Jeter Publishing.

Colvin, Geoff. 2021. "The Super Bowl Proves It: The NFL Rules the Television World." *Fortune*, February 6, 2021.

Connell, R. W., and James W. Messerschmidt. 2005. "Hegemonic Masculinity: Rethinking the Concept." *Gender and Society* 19 (6): 829–859.

Considine, Tim. 1982. *The Language of Sport*. New York: World Almanac.

Cook, Kevin. 2012. *The Last Headbangers: NFL Football in the Rowdy, Reckless '70s: The Era That Created Modern Sports*. New York: W. W. Norton.

Cooper, Roger, and Tang Tang. 2018. "Gender and Predictors of Multiplatform Media Uses: A Case Study of the Super Bowl." *International Journal of Sport Communication* 6 (3): 348–363.

Costa, Brandon. 2019, December 19. *Fox Sports will produce Super Bowl LIV in 1080p HDR*. Sports Video Blog.

Craig, Roger, and Matt Maiocco. 2012. *Tales from the San Francisco 49ers Sideline: A Collection of the Greatest 49ers Stories Ever Told.* La Vergne, TN: Sports Publishing.

Cranmer, Ziba. 2011. "The Silent Sports Trade: Sex Trafficking." *Changemakers.com*, March 3, 2011.

Crepeau, Richard. 2014. *NFL Football: A History of America's New National Pastime.* Urbana: University of Illinois Press.

Crepeau, Richard. 2017. "The Super Bowl at 50 or L." *International Journal of the History of Sport* 34 (1–2): 7–22.

Cresswell, Julie. 2021. "Super Bowl Means Snacking, Even without Parties." *New York Times*, February 8, 2021.

Crouch, Ian. 2017. "The Best and Worst 2017 Super Bowl Ads." *New Yorker*, February 5, 2017.

Culverhouse, Gay. 2011. *Throwaway Players: Concussion Crisis from Pee Wee Football to the NFL.* Lake Forest, CA: Behler Publications.

D'Addario, Daniel. 2018. "At the Super Bowl, Justin Timberlake Plays a High-Stakes Game." *Time*, February 12, 2018.

Daley, Robert. 1968. *Only a Game: The Novel that Snooked the Pro Football World.* Signet.

Danzig, Allison. 1956. *The History of American Football.* Englewood Cliffs, NJ: Prentice Hall.

Davis, Laurel R. 1997. *The Swimsuit Issue and Sport: Hegemonic Masculinity in Sports Illustrated.* Ithaca: State University of New York Press.

Dawidoff, Nicholas. 2013. *Collision Low Crossers: A Year inside the Turbulent World of NFL Football.* New York: Little, Brown.

Dearing, Ronda L., Cheryl Twaragowski, Philip H. Smith, Gregory G. Homish, Gerard J. Connors, and Kimberly S. Walitzer. 2014. "Super Bowl Sunday: Risky Business for At-Risk (Male) Drinkers?" nih.gov, March 12, 2014.

Deford, Frank. 1981. *Everybody's All-American.* New York: Signet

Deford, Frank. 2009. "Super Bowl Is the New U. S. Holiday." *Arizona Daily Star*, February 1, 2009. http://www.azstarnet.com/opinion/278142.

Dheensaw, Cleve. 2015. Interview with Michael Real. *Victoria Times Colonist*. February 1, 2015

Didinger, Ray. 1990. *The Super Bowl: Celebrating a Quarter-Century of America's Greatest Game.* New York: Simon and Schuster.

DeLillo, Don. 1972. *End Zone.* Boston: Houghton Mifflin.

DeLillo, Don. 2020. *The Silence: A Novel.* New York: Scribner.

Dent, Jim. 2011. *Super Bowl Texas Style.* Roughneck Media

Dimon, Laura. 2014. "This Is the Dark Side of the Super Bowl You'll Never See on TV." Mic.com/articles 79235, January 27, 2014.

Didinger, Ray. 1990. *The Super Bowl: Celebrating a Quarter-Century of America's Greatest Game.* New York: Simon and Schuster.

Doan, Paul. 2019. "Toxic Masculinity and Super Bowl Advertising." Communication Studies Undergraduate Publications 94, University of Portland.

Doeden, Matt. 2017. *The Super Bowl: Chasing Football Immortality.* Minneapolis, MN: Millbrook Press.

Drape, Joe. 2019. "Sports Betting: An Emerging National Pastime." *New York Times*, January 30, 2019.

Drape, Joe, and Tiffany Hsu. 2021. "Calling a Reverse, the NFL Embraces Ads for Gambling." *New York Times*, September 16, 2021.

Drenten, Jenna, Cara O. Peters, Thomas Leigh, and Candice Hollenbeck. 2009. "Not Just a Party in the Parking Lot: An Exploratory Investigation of the Motives Underlying the Ritual Commitment of Football Tailgaters." *Sport Marketing Quarterly* 18 (2): 92–106.

Drozda, Joe. 1996. *The Tailgater's Handbook*. Knoxville, TN: Masters Press.

Duncan, Margaret Carlisle, and Alan Aycock. 2008. "'I Laughed until I Hurt': Negative Humor in Super Bowl Ads." In *Sport, Beer, and Gender: Promotional Culture and Contemporary Social Life*, edited by Lawrence A. Wenner and Steven J. Jackson, 243–260. New York: Peter Lang Publishers.

Dunning, Eric. 2003. "Sociological Reflections on Sport, Violence and Civilization." In *Sport: Critical Concepts in Sociology*, edited by Eric Dunning and Dominic Malcolm, 41–59. London: Routledge.

Dutton, Jack. 2021. "Over 70 Arrested in Florida Prostitution Sting Ahead of Super Bowl LV." *Newsweek*, January 12, 2021.

Easterbrook, Greg. 2005. "Don't Analyze That: A Day of Excess Won't Kill Us." *New York Times*, February 6, 2005: D7.

Easterbrook, Gregg. 2013. *The King of Sports: Football's Impact on America*. New York: Thomas Dunne Books.

Editors of *Sports Illustrated*. 2015. Super Bowl Gold: 50 Years of the Big Game. *Sports Illustrated*.

Ehrenreich, Barbara. 2006. *Dancing in the Streets: A History of Collective Joy*. New York: Metropolitan Books.

Eichelberger, Curtis. 2012. *Men of Sunday: How Faith Guides the Players, Coaches, and Wives of the NFL*. Nashville, TN: Thomas Nelson.

Eisenberg, John. 2012. *Ten-Gallon War: The NFL's Cowboys, the AFL's Texans, and the Feud for Dallas's Pro Football Future*. Boston: Houghton Mifflin Harcourt.

Eisenberg, John. 2018. *The League: How Five Rivals Created the NFL and Launched a Sports Empire*. New York: Basic Books.

Eitzen, Stanley D. 2016. *Fair and Foul: Beyond the Myths and Paradoxes of Sport*. 6th ed. New York: Rowman & Littlefield.

El-Bawab, Nadine. 2021. "Super Bowl LV Tickets Can Cost up to $40,000—And Only 14,500 Are Available to Buy." CNBC.com, February 2, 2021.

Elyot, Thomas. 1531. *The Boke Named the Governour*. Royal Collection Trust, UK.

Ember, Sydney. 2016. "Super Bowl Ads Play It Safe, Sticking to the Script." *New York Times*, February 7, 2016.

Esmonde, Katelyn. 2017. "Sexism and the Super Bowl: What Can We Learn from Female Sports Fans?" *Engaging Sports*/Thesocietypages.org, February 2, 2017.

Fabrizio, Daniel and Jim Cee. 2010. *Sports Investing: NFL Betting Systems*. BCDadvisors.

Fainaru-Wada, Mark, and Steve Fainaru. 2013. *League of Denial: The NFL, Concussions and the Battle for Truth*. New York: Crown Archetype.

Feeney, Nolan. 2014. "The Legacy of Janet Jackson's Boob." *Atlantic*, January 31, 2014.

Feinstein, John. 2008. *Cover-Up*. New York: Yearling Books.

Felser, Larry. 2008. *The Birth of the New NFL: How the 1966 NFL/AFL Merger Transformed Pro Football*. Guilford, CT: Lyons Press.

Femina, Jerry Della. 2001. "The final score: Beer 21, dot coms 0." *Wall Street Journal*: A14.

Fera, Rae Ann. 2013. "4 Reasons Why Pre-Game Content Is a Winning Super Bowl Strategy." *Fast Company*, January 30, 2013.

Fischer, David. 2015. *The Super Bowl: The First Fifty Years of America's Greatest Game*. New York: Sports Publishing.

Fischer, Mia. 2014. "Commemorating 9/11 NFL-Style: Insights into America's Culture of Militarism." *Journal of Sport and Social Issues* 38 (3): 199–221.

Fleder, Rob, ed. 2019. *NFL 100: A Century of Pro Football*. New York: Abrams Books.

Fleischer, Ari. 2017. "Too any flags in Trump's first quarter." *Wall Street Journal*, December 27.

Flint, Joe. 2011. "How the NFL Turned the Super Bowl into a Phenomenon." *Los Angeles Times*, February 4, 2011.

Forney, Craig A. 2007. *The Holy Trinity of American Sports: Civil Religion in Football, Baseball, and Basketball*. Macon, GA: Mercer University Press.

Francisco, Frank. 2016. *Evolution of the Game: A Chronicle of American Football*. Scotts Valley, CA: Create Space Independent Publishing Platform.

Fredericks, Jennifer E. 2016. "Sex Trafficking and the Super Bowl: A Connection between Major Sporting Events and Human Trafficking." Unpublished Master's thesis, Ridge College of Intelligence Studies and Applied Sciences, Mercyhurst University.

Freeman, Mike. 2012. *Undefeated: Inside the 1972 Miami Dolphins' Perfect Season*. New York: It Books.

Freeman, Mike. 2020. *Football's Fearless Activists: How Colin Kaepernick, Eric Reid, Kenny Stills, and Fellow Athletes Stood up to the NFL and President Trump*. New York: Sports Publishing.

Frommer, Harvey. 2015. *When It Was Just a Game: Remembering the First Super Bowl*. Lanham, MD: Taylor Trade Publishing.

Fulks, Matt. 2008. *The Good, the Bad & the Ugly: Heart-Pounding, Jaw-Dropping, and Gut-Wrenching Moments from Pittsburgh Steelers History*. Chicago: Triumph Books.

Fuller, Linda K. 1992. *Sportstalk/Wartalk/Patriotismtalk/Mentalk: Super Bowl XXV*, paper presented at the International Association for Mass Communication Research conference, Guaruja, Brazil.

Fuller, Linda K. 1999. "Super Bowl Speak: Subtexts of Sex and Sex Talk in America's Annual Sports Extravaganza." In *Sexual Rhetoric: Media Perspectives on Sexuality, Gender, and Identity*, edited by M. G. Carstarphen and S. C. Zavoina, 161–173. Westport, CT: Greenwood Press.

Fuller, Linda K. 2004. "Fictionalizing (American) Football: A Case Study of the TV Show *Playmakers*." Porto Alegra, Brazil: International Association for Media and Communication Research.

Fuller, Linda K (ed.). 2006. *Sport, Rhetoric, and Gender: Historical Perspectives and Media Representations*. New York: Palgrave Macmillan.

Fuller, Linda K. 2007a. "Pat Tillman: Sport Hero/Martyr as Militaristic Symbol of the Iraq/Afghanistan War." Presented at the International Association for Media and Communication Research 50th Anniversary Conference, Paris.

Fuller, Linda K. 2007b. "The Spicy, Gendered Language of Sport." Paper Presented to the National Communication Association, Chicago, IL.

Fuller, Linda K. 2008. *Sportscasters/Sportscasting: Practices and Principles*. New York: Routledge.

Fuller, Linda K. 2009. "Foreword: Sport Communication Linked with Linguistics." In Barry Brummett (Ed.). 2009. *Sporting Rhetoric: Performance, Games, and Politics*, ix-xi. NY: Peter Lang.

Fuller, Linda K. 2010. "Foul Language: A Feminist Perspective on (American) Football Film Rhetoric." In *Sexual Sport Rhetoric: Historical and Media Contexts of Violence*, edited by Linda K. Fuller, 179–192. New York: Peter Lang.

Fuller, Linda K. 2015. *Bad Boys and Good Old Boys in the Ray Rice Assault Case*. New Orleans, LA: Popular Culture Association.

Fulks, Matt. 2008. *The Good, the Bad & the Ugly: Heart-Pounding, Jaw-Dropping, and Gut-Wrenching Moments from Pittsburgh Steelers History*. Chicago: Triumph Books.

Gagnier, Suzanna. 2007. *Putting on the Blitz: The Football Book for Women*. Action Press.

Gallagher, Pat, and Stephanie Martin. 2017. *Big Game, Bigger Impact: How the Bay Area Redefined the Super Bowl Experience and the Lessons That Can Apply to Any Business*. Melbourne, FL: Motivational Press.

Gantz, Walter, Zheng Wang, and Samuel D. Bradley. 2006. "Televised NFL Games, the Family, and Domestic Violence." In *Handbook of Sports and Media*, edited by Arthur A. Raney and Jennings Bryant, 365–381. Mahwah, NJ: Lawrence Erlbaum Associates.

Gargano, Anthony L. 2010. *NFL Unplugged: The Brutal, Brilliant World of Professional Football*. Hoboken, NJ: Wiley.

Gellman, Wendy. 2013. "Super Bowl Sunday Now Recognized as Jewish Holiday." *Huffington Post*, April 5, 2013.

Gems, Gerald R. 2000. *For Pride, Profit, and Patriarchy: Football and the Incorporation of American Cultural Values*. Lanham, MD: Scarecrow Press.

Gems, Gerald R., and Gertrud Pfister. 2009. *Understanding American Sports*. London: Routledge.

Gems, Gerald R., and Gertrud Pfister, eds. 2019. *Touchdown: An American Obsession Goes Global*. Great Barrington, MA: Berkshire Publishing.

Gent, Peter. 1973. *North Dallas forty*. Total/Sports Illustrated.

Geyerman, Chris B. 2016. "The NFL's "Violence against Women Problem": Media Framing and the Perpetuation of Domestic Abuse." *Studies in Popular Culture* 38 (2): 99–124.

Gifford, Frank, and Peter Richmond. 2008. *The Glory Game: How the 1958 NFL Championship Changed Football Forever*. Pymble, Australia: HarperCollins.

Gilden, Jack. 2018. *From the Desk of Jack Gilden: Sports in Context*. Pigskin Books.

Giorgis, Hannah. 2020. "The NFL's Most Valued Cause Is Itself." *Atlantic*, February 3, 2020.

Glauber, Bob. 2018. *Guts and Genius: The Story of Three Unlikely Coaches who Came to Dominate the NFL in the '80s*. New York: Grand Central Publishing.

Glennon, Sean. 2012. *Tom Brady vs. the NFL: The Case for Football's Greatest Quarterback*. Chicago: Triumph Books.

Gordon, Dan. 2008. *Beat the Sports Books: An Insider's Guide to Betting the NFL*, 2nd ed. Las Vegas, NV: Cardoza.

Gordon, Aaron. 2015. "*Playmakers*, the Show the NFL Killed for Being too Real." vice.com, April 22, 2015.

Gordon, Roger. 2017. *So You Think You're a Cleveland Browns Fan?: Stars, Stats, Records, and Memories for True Diehards*. New York: Sports Publishing.

Graham, Carl O. 2019. "Domestic Violence and the Super Bowl." Graham. law, February 4, 2019.

Graham, Megan, and Jabari Young. 2020. "Women Are Watching the NFL in Record Numbers, and Super Bowls Are Finally Starting to Reflect That." CNBC.com, February 2, 2020.

Green, Jerry. 1991. *Super Bowl Chronicles: A Sportswriter Reflects on the First 25 Years of America's Game*. Grand Rapids, MI: Masters Press.

Green, Kyle, and Madison Van Oort. 2013. "'We Wear No Pants': Selling the Crisis of Masculinity in the 2010 Super Bowl Commercials." *Signs* 38 (3): 695–719.

Green, Sarah A. 2011. *Football, the Basics for Women*. Kenner, LA: Destiny Publishing.

Gregory, Sean. 2009. "Thrown for a Loss: Super Bowl Parties." Time.com, January 28, 2009.

Griffith, R. D. 2012. *To the NFL: You Sure Started Somethin': A Historical Guide of All 32 NFL Teams and the Cities They've Played in*. Pittsburgh, PA: Dorrance Publishing.

Grindstaff, Laura, and Emily West. 2006. "Cheerleading and the Gendered Politics of Sport." *Social Problems* 53 (4): 500–518.

Gruver, Ed, and Jim Campbell. 2019. *Hell with the Lid Off: Inside the Fierce Rivalry between the 1970s Oakland Raiders and Pittsburgh Steelers*. Lincoln: University of Nebraska Press.

Hadro, Matt. 2015. "The Dark Side of the Super Bowl: Sex Trafficking." *National Catholic Register*, January 28, 2015.

Hagood, Mack, and Travis Vogan. 2016. "The 12th Man: Fan Noise in the Contemporary NFL." *Popular Communication* 14 (1): 3–38.

Hall, Willian III. 2013. *Get In and Win Pro Football Playbook: For Predicting Scores and Placing Winner Wagers By a Wall Street Investment Manager*. Bookworm Sports.

Hanlon, Patrick. 2014. "Apple '1984' Spot Won the Game 30 Super Bowls Ago." *Forbes*, January 30, 2014.

Hanson, Mary Ellen. 1995. *Go! Fight! Win!: Cheerleading in American Culture*. Madison: University of Wisconsin Press.

Haring, Bruce. 2020. "Super Bowl LV May Double Down on Social and Racial Justice Ads." Deadline.com, December 5, 2020.

Harris, David. 1986. *The League: The Rise and Decline of the NFL*. Toronto, Canada: Bantam Books.

Harris, David. 2018. *The Genius: How Bill Walsh Reinvented Football and Created an NFL Dynasty*. New York: Random House.

Harris, John M. 2018. *Redemption in '64: The Champion Cleveland Browns*. Kent, Ohio: The Kent State University Press.

Hayward, George M., and Anna Rybinska. 2017. "'Super Bowl Babies': Do Countries with Super Bowl Winning Teams Experience Increases in Births Nine Months Later?" *Socius: Sociological Research for a Dynamic World* 3:1–14.

Henseler, Kylea. 2020. "Super Bowl Economic Impact Touches Down at $571 Million." *Miami Today*, October 27, 2020.

Herget, James E. 2013. *American Football: How the Game Evolved*. Scotts Valley, CA: Create Space Independent Publishing Platform.

Higgs, Robert J., and Michael Braswell. 2004. *An Unholy Alliance: The Sacred and Modern Sports*. Macon, GA: Mercer University Press.

Hindman, Lauren C., and Nefertiti A. Walker. 2021. "Feminine and Sexy: A Feminist Critical Discourse Analysis of Gender Ideology and Professional Cheerleading." *Journal of Sport Management* September:1–15.

Hoge, Merril. 2018. *Brainwashed: The Bad Science behind CTE and the Plot to Destroy Football*. Virginia: Mascot Books.

Holley, Michael. 2005. *Patriot Reign: Bill Belichick, the Coaches, and the Players Who Built a Champion*. New York: It Books.

Holley, Michael. 2012. *War Room: The Legacy of Bill Belichick and the Art of Building the Perfect Team*. New York: It Books.

Hopsicker, Peter, and Mark Dyreson. 2017. "Super Bowl Sunday: A National Holiday and a Global Curiosity." *International Journal of the History of Sport* 34 (1): 1–6.

Horovitz, Bruce. 2009. "Two Nobodies from Nowhere" Craft Winning Ad. *USA Today*, February 2, 2009:4B.

Horrigan, Joe. 2019. *NFL Century: The One-Hundred-Year Rise of America's Greatest Sports League*. New York: Random House.

Horrow, Rick, and Karla Swatek. 2011. *Beyond the Scoreboard: An Insider's Guide to the Business of Sport*. Champaign, IL: Human Kinetics.

Huebenthal, Jan. 2013. "'Quick! Do Something Manly!': The Super Bowl as an American Spectacle of Hegemonic Masculinity, Violence, and Nationalism." Dissertations, Theses, and Masters Projects, College of William & Mary.

James, Jeffrey, Steven G. Breezeel, and Stephen Ross. 2011. "A Two-Stage Study of the Reasons to Begin and Continue Tailgating." *Sports Marketing Quarterly* 10 (4): 212–223.

Jaworski, Ron, David Plaut, and Greg Cosell. 2010. *The Games That Changed the Game: The Evolution of the NFL in Seven Sundays*. New York: ESPN.

Jenkins, Dan. 1977. *Semi-Tough*. Boston: Da Capo Press.

Jenkins, Henry. 2006. *Convergence Culture: Where Old and New Media Collide*. New York: New York University Press.

Jenkins, Sally. 1996. *Men Will Be Boys: The Modern Woman Explains Football and Other Amusing Male Rituals*. New York: Doubleday.

Jhally, Sut. 2018. *Advertising at the Edge of the Apocalypse*. Northampton, MA: Media Education Foundation

Johnson, Pableaux. 2007. *ESPN Gameday Gourmet: More than 80 All-American Tailgate Recipes*. ESPN

Jones, Jack. 2021. "How Much Money Is Bet on the Super Bowl?" Betfirm. com, April 8, 2021.

Jonsson, Patrick. 2021. "Cooking for 15,000: How Fort Bragg Pulls Off Thanksgiving." *Christian Science Monitor*, November 24, 2021.

Jozsa, Frank P., Jr. 2010. *Football Fortunes: The Business, Organization and Strategy of the NFL*. London: MacFarland.

Kaleem, Jaweed. 2014. "Half of Americans Say God Plays a Role in Super Bowl Winner." Citywatchla.com, January 16, 2014.

Kanner, Bernice. 2004. *The Super Bowl of Advertising: How the Commercials Won the Game*. Princeton, NJ: Bloomberg Press.

Kellner, Douglas. 2003. *Media Spectacle*. London: Routledge.

King, C. Richard. 2010. "Hail to the Chiefs: Race, Gender, and Native American Sports Mascots." In *Sexual Sports Rhetoric: Historical and Media Contexts of Violence*, edited by Linda K. Fuller, 193–203. New York: Peter Lang.

King, C. Richard. 2016. *Redskins: Insult and Brand*. Lincoln: University of Nebraska Press.

King, C. Richard, and Charles Frueling Springwood, eds. 2001. *Team Spirits: The Native American Mascot Controversy*. University of Nebraska Press.

Knight, Jonathan. 2003. *Kardiac Kids: The Story of the 1980 Cleveland Browns*. Ohio, Kent: The Kent State University Press.

Knight, Jonathan. 2006. *Sundays in the Pound: The Heroics and Heartbreak of the 1985-89 Cleveland Browns*. Ohio, Kent: The Kent State University Press.

Knight, Jonathan. 2015. *Classic Browns: The 50 Greatest Games in Cleveland Browns History*. 2nd ed. Ohio, Kent: The Kent State University Press.

Kobrin, Mindy. n.d. "Super Bowl Halftime Blitz Party." http://www.celebrations.com/article/Super-Bowl-Halftime-Blitz-Party.

Kounalakis, Markos. 2020. "The Ugly History of the Super Bowl Teams' Mascots." *Washington Monthly*, February 5, 2020.

Konik, Michael. 2008. *The Smart Money: How the World's Best Sports Bettors Beat the Bookies Out of Millions*. New York: Simon & Schuster.

Krakauer, Jon. 2010. *Where Men Win Glory: The Odyssey of Pat Tillman*. New York: Anchor Books.

Krattenmaker, Tom. 2019. "Super Bowl's Old-School Masculinity Needs an Update: Real Men Get Help When They Need It." *USA Today*, February 1, 2019.

Kriegel, Mark. 2004. *Namath: A biography*. New York, Penguin Books.

Lampe, Ray ("Dr. BBQ"). 2008. *The NFL gameday cookbook: 150 recipes to feed the hungriest fan from preseason to the Super Bowl*. San Francisco, CA: Chronicle Books.

Lapchick, Richard. 2020. "The Super Bowl Remains Target for Human Trafficking." ESPN.com, January 31, 2020.

Lazarus, Adam. 2012. *Best of Rivals: Joe Montana, Steve Young, and the Inside Story Behind the NFL's Greatest Quarterback Controversy*. Cambridge, MA: Da Capo Press.

Leibovich, Mark. 2018. *Big Game: The NFL in Dangerous Times*. New York: Penguin.

Leiger, Neil. 2011. *Guts and Glory: The Golden Age of American Football*. Los Angeles, CA: Taschen.

Lewis, Michael. 2007. *The Blind Side: Evolution of a Game*. New York: W. W. Norton & Company.

Library of Congress and Susan Reyburn. 2013. *Football Nation: Four Hundred Years of America's Game*. New York: Harry N. Abrams.

Lombardi, Vince, Jr. 2004. *The Lombardi Rules: 26 Lessons from Vince Lombardi—The World's Greatest Coach*. New York: McGraw-Hill.

Lupro, Michael Mooradian. 2013. "The Super in the Super Bowl." In *American History through American Sports: Sports at the Center of Popular Culture: The Television Age*, edited by Danielle Sarver Coombs and Bob Batchelor, 93–102. Santa Barbara, CA: Praeger.

Lydecker, Janet A., Antonio Izzo, Gail Spielberger, and Carlos M. Grilo. 2017. " 'I Only Watch for the Commercials': Messages and Weight, Eating and Race in Super Bowl Advertisements." *International Journal of Clinical Practice* 1 (11): e13026.

MacCambridge, Michael. 2005. *America's Game: The Epic Story of How Pro Football Captured a Nation*. New York: Anchor.

Madden, John. 1988. *Ultimate Tailgating*. New York: Viking.

Magary, Drew. 2009. *20 Rules for Your Super Bowl Party*. Deadspin.com, January 29, 2009.

Maki, Allan, and Dave Naylor. 2016. *50 Super Bowls: The Greatest Moments of the Biggest Game in Sport*s. Buffalo, NY: Firefly Books.

Malamuet, Melissa. 2010. *She's Got Game: The Woman's Guide to Loving Sports (or Just How to Fake It!)*. New York: St. Martin's Griffin.

Mandelbaum, Michael. 2020. "The Meaning of the Super Bowl." *American Interest*, February 2, 2020.

Manfredo, Augie. 2012. *How I Made Money Betting NFL Football*. CreateSpace Independent Publishing Platform.

Martin, Lauren, and Annie Hill. 2019. "Debunking the Myth of 'Super Bowl Sex Trafficking': Media Hype or Evidenced-Based Coverage." *Anti-Trafficking Review* 13:13–29.

Matchar, Emily. 2009. "Slashfood: A Very Martha Stewart Super Bowl Party." January 26, 2009. http://www.slashfood.com/2009/01/26/a-very-martha-stewart-super-bowl-party.

McAllister, Matthew P. 2003. "Is Commercial Culture Popular Culture?: A Question for Popular Communication Scholars." *Popular Communication* 1 (1): 41–49.

McAllister, Matthew P., and Elysia Galindo-Ramirez. 2017. "Fifty Years of Super Bowl Commercials, Thirty-Two Years of Spectacular Consumption." *International Journal of the History of Sport* 34:46–64.

McDowell, Jacqueline, and Spencer Schaffner. 2011. "Football, It's a Man's Game: Insult and Gendered Discourse." *Gender Bowl: Discourse & Society* 22 (5): 547–564.

McGinn, Bob. 2012. *The Ultimate Super Bowl Book: A Complete Reference to the Stats, Stars, and Stories Behind Football's Biggest Game—And Why the Best Team Won.* 2nd ed. Minneapolis, MN: MVP Books.

McGown, Tom. 2013. "NFL Cheerleaders: Gratuitous Sexism or All-American Fun?". *CNN.*

McGregor, Jena. 2014. "Indra Nooyi, the NFL and the 'Responsibility' of Female CEOs." *Washington Post*, September 19. Available: http://www.washingtonpost.com/blogs/on-leadership/wp/2014/09/19/indra-nooyi-the-nfl-and-the-responsibility-of-female-ceos/

McIntire, David. 2013. *Swimming with the Sharps: A Football Season Spent in Las Vegas.* Outskirts Press.

Meggyesy, Dave. 1970. *Out of Their League.* Bison Books.

Messner, Michael A. 1992. *Power at Play: Sports and the Problem of Masculinity.* Boston: Beacon Press.

Messner, Michael A. 1997. *Politics of Masculinities: Men in Movements.* Thousand Oaks, CA: Sage.

Messner, Michael A. 2002. *Taking the Field: Women, Men, and Sport.* Minneapolis: University of Minnesota Press.

Messner, Michael A., and Don Sabo, eds. 1990. *Sport, Men, and the Gender Order: Critical Feminist Perspectives.* Champaign, IL: Human Kinetics Books.

Messner, Michael A., and Jeffrey Montez de Oca. 2005. "The Male Consumer as Loser: Beer and Liquor Ads in Mega Sports Media Events." *Signs* 30 (3): 1879–1909.

Miller, John, Frank Veltri, and Any Gillentine. 2008. "Spectator Perceptions of Security at the Super Bowl after 9/11: Implications for Sport Facility Managers." *Smart Journal* 4 (2): 16–25.

Minsberg, Talya. 2021. "Have Yourself a Ball on Super Bowl Sunday." *New York Times*, January 31, 2021: D4.

Morris, Benjamin. 2014a. "The Rate of Domestic Violence Arrests among NFL Players." *FiveThirtyEight*, July 31, 2014.

Morris, Benjamin. 2014b. "More on the Rate of Domestic Violence Arrests among NFL Players." *FiveThirtyEight*, October 2, 2014.

Moskowitz, Tobias, and L. Jon Wertheim. 2012. *Scorecasting: The Hidden Influences behind How Sports Are Played and Games Are Won.* New York: Three Rivers Press.

Moose, Debbie. 2007. *Fan Fare: A Playbook of Great Recipes for Tailgating or Watching the Game at Home.* Boston: Harvard Common Press.

Mullen, Lawrence J., and Dennis W. Mazzocco. 2000. "Coaches, Drama, and Technology: Mediation of Super Bowl Broadcasts from 1969 to 1997." *Critical Studies in Media Communication* 17 (3): 347–363.

Murphy, Kasie. 2020. "The X League: An Illegal Hold on Women's Sporting Possibilities." thesocietypages.org/engagingsports, March 5, 2020.

Nelson, David. 1994. *Anatomy of a Game: Football, the Rules and the Men Who Made the Game*. Newark, Delaware: University of Delaware Press.

Nelson, Mariah Burton. 1994. *The Stronger Women Get, the More Men Love Football: Sexism and the American Culture of Sports*. Harcourt Brace.

Newell, A. J. 2012. *Gaga for Gridiron: The Ultimate Guide to Football for Women*. 2nd ed. Scotts Valley, CA: Create Space Independent Publishing Platform.

Nicholas, Alice. 2007. *Talk Football: Written by a Woman for Women Who Want to Speak America's Gridiron Language*. Jackson, Mississippi: Pecan Row Press.

Niman, Michael I. 2006. "Who Killed Pat Tillman?" *Humanist*, January/February.

Norwood, Stephen H. 2019. *New York Sports*. Arkansas: University of Arkansas Press.

Nyland, David. 2007. *Beer, Babes, and Balls: Masculinity and Sports Talk Radio*. Albany, NY: SUNY Press.

Oates, Thomas P. 2017. *Football and Manliness: An Unauthorized Account of the NFL*. Urbana: University of Illinois Press.

Oates, Thomas P., and Zack Furness, eds. 2014. *The NFL: Critical and Cultural Perspectives*. Philadelphia, Pennsylvania: Temple University Press.

O'Donnell, Hugh, and Robert Spires. 2008. "America at Play, America at War: The Super Bowl as Discursive Formation." *Comunicação Pública* 3 (6): 53–72.

Olesker, Michael. 2008. *The Colts' Baltimore: A City and its Love Affair in the 1950s*. Baltimore, Maryland: John Hopkins University Press

Olmsted, Larry. 2021. "The Lessons We Can Learn from Sports Fandom: There's a Reason Why Loyalty Is Especially Fierce in One Realm." *New York Daily News*, February 4, 2021.

O'Neal, Sean. 2021. "'Necessary Roughness' Made Texas Football into a Joke: But It Also Moved the Chains." *Texas Monthly*, September 14, 2021.

Oriard, Michael. 1998. *Reading Football: How the Popular Press Created an American Spectacle*. Chapel Hill: University of North Carolina Press.

Oriard, Michael. 2010. *Brand NFL: Making and Selling America's Favorite Sport*. Chapel Hill: University of North Carolina Press.

Osborne, Anne Cunningham, and Danielle Sarver Coombs. 2016. *Female Fans of the NFL: Taking Their Place in the Stands*. New York: Routledge.

Patoski, Joe Nick. 2012. *The Dallas Cowboys: The Outrageous History of the Biggest, Loudest, Most Hated, Best Loved Football Team in America*. New York: Little, Brown.

Pearlman, Jeff. 2009. *Boys Will Be Boys: The Glory Days and Party Nights of the Dallas Cowboys Dynasty*. New York: Harper Perennial.

Peete, Holly Robinson, and Daniel Paisner. 2005. *Get Your Own Damn Beer, I'm Watching the Game! A Woman's Guide to Loving Pro Football*. Pennsylvania: Rodale Press.

Perry, Stephen D., ed. 2019. *Pro Football and the Proliferation of Protest: Anthem Posture in a Divided America*. Maryland: Lexington Books.

Peterson, Beth. 2018. *The Tailgate Cookbook: 75 Game-Changing Recipes for the Tastiest Tailgate Ever*. Springville, UT: Front Table Books.

Peterson, Robert W. 1997. *Pigskin: The Early Years of Pro Football*. New York: Oxford University Press.

Pilato, Donna. 2009. "Planning Your Super Bowl Party." http://entertaining.about.com/cs/superbowlsunday/a/superbowl_2.htm?p=1.

Pinak, Patrick. 2021. "Roger Goodell's Net Worth: How Rich Is the NFL Commissioner?" fanbuzz.com, February 2, 2021.

Polian, Bill, and Vic Carucci. 2021. *Super Bowl Blueprints: Hall of Famers Reveal the Keys to Football's Greatest Dynasties*. Chicago: Triumph Books.

Price, Joseph L. 1982. "The Super Bowl as Religious Festival." *Christian Century*, February 22, 1982.

Price, Joseph L., ed. 2001. *From Season to Season: Sports as American Religion*. Macon, GA: Mercer University Press.

Queenan, Joe. 2009. "Super Bowl Suits." *New York Times*, January 30, 2009.

Quindlen, Anna. 1993. *Time to Tackle This*. The New York Times, January 17.

Rappoport, Ken. 2010. *The Little League That Could: A History of the American Football League*. Blue Ridge Summit, PA: Taylor Trade Publishing.

Ratajkowski, Emily. 2021. *My Body*. New York: Metropolitan Books.

Real, Michael R. 1975. "The Super Bowl: Mythic Spectacle." *Journal of Communication* 75:31–45.

Real, Michael R. 1989. "Super Bowl Football versus World Cup Soccer: A Cultural-Structural Comparison." In *Media, Sports, and Society*, edited by Lawrence A. Wenner, 180–203. Thousand Oaks, CA: Sage.

Real, Michael R. 1995. "The Super Bowl: Mythic Spectacle" In Newcomb, Horace (Ed),
    Television: The Critical View, 170-203. New York: Oxford University Press.

Real, Michael R. 1998. Technology and the commodification of postmodern sport. In *MediaSport*, edited by Lawrence A. Wenner,14-26. New York: Routledge.

Real, Michael R. 2013. "Reflections on Communication and Sport: On Spectacle and Mega-Events." *Communication & Sport*, January 16, 2013:1–30.

Real, Michael R., and Lawrence A. Wenner. 2017. "Super Bowl: Mythic Spectacle Revisited." In *Sport, Media and Mega-Events*, edited by Lawrence A. Wenner and Andrew C. Billings, 199–217. New York: Routledge.

Reed, Eric. 2020. "Super Bowl Revenue: How Much Does the Big Game Generate?" *USA Today*, January 20, 2020.

Reimer, Alex. 2020. "Super Bowl 54 Was Most Political in History." *Forbes*, February 3, 2020.

Revsine, Dave. 2014. *The Opening Kickoff: The Tumultuous Birth of a Football Nation*. Guilford, CT: Lyons Press.

Rice, Jerry, and Randy O. Williams. 2019. *America's Game: The NFL at 100*. New York: HarperCollins.

Ritter, Malcolm. 2008. "For Die-Hard Fans, Super Bowl May Literally Be Heartbreaking." Pantagraph.com, January 30, 2008.

Rivers, Francine. 2016. "The Dark Side of the Super Bowl." *Francine's Newsletter*. Available: https://francinerivers.com/the-dark-side-of-the-super-bowl.

Rockwell, Ashley M. 2016. "A Shift in Gender Representations and Narratives in Super Bowl Commercials." Unpublished thesis, Department of Sociology, Georgia State University.

Rosenberg, Howard. 1991. "Hussein—A Football Fan?" *Los Angeles Times*, January 28, 1991.

Rozell, Pete. 1991. *Super Bowl: Celebrating a Quarter Century of America's Greatest Game*. New York: Random House.

Rugg, Adam. 2019. "Incorporating the Protests: The NFL, Social Justice, and the Constrained Activism of the 'Inspire Change' Campaign." *Communication & Sport* 8 (4–5): 611–628.

Russell, Ryan. 2021. "The Trouble with the NFL." *New York Times*, October 17, 2021:SR7.

Sabo, Don F., and Joe Panepinto. 1990. In *Sport, Men, and the Gender Order: Critical Feminist Perspectives*, edited by Michael Messner and Don F. Sabo, 115–126. Champaign, IL: Human Kinetics.

Sandomir, Richard. 2009. "How Jackson Redefined the Super Bowl." *New York Times*, June 29, 2009.

Saucedo-Artino, Teresa. 2000. *Football for Females: The Women's Survival Guide to the Football Season*. Pittsburgh, PA: Dorrance Publishing.

Scheaffer, Ann. 2019. *Tailgating Done Right Cookbook: 150 Recipes for a Winning Game Day*. Mount Joy, PA: Fox Chapel.

Schwartz, Dona. 1997. *Contesting the Super Bowl*. New York: Routledge.

Segrave, Jeffrey O. 1997. "A Matter of Life and Death: Some Thoughts on the Language of Sport." *Journal of Sport & Social Issues* 21 (12): 211–220.

Semuels, Alana. 2019. "The White Flight from Football." *Atlantic*, February 1, 2019.

Simms, Phil, and Vic Carucci. 2005. *Sunday Morning Quarterback: Going Deep on the Strategies, Myths, and Mayhem of Football*. New York: It Books.

Sloan, Robert. 2005. *Tailgating Cookbook: Recipes for the Big Game*. San Francisco, CA: Chronicle Books.

Smith, Dean. 2013. *Never Easy, Never Pretty: A Fan, a City, a Championship Season*. Maryland: John Hopkins University Press.

Smith, Bobby. 2008. *How to Beat the Pro Football Pointspread: A Comprehensive, No-Nonsense Guide to Picking NFL Winners*. New York: Skyhorse.

Sobal, Jeffrey. 2006. "Men, Meat, and Marriage: Models of Masculinity." *Food and Foodways: Explorations in the History and Culture of Human Nourishment* 13 (1–2): 135–158.

Solotaroff, Paul. 2011. "Dave Duerson: The Ferocious Life and Tragic Death of a Super Bowl Star." *Men's Journal*, February 2011.

Sperber, Murray. 2001. *Beer and Circus: How Big-Time College Sports is Crippling Undergraduate Education*. New York: Henry Holt.

Staurowsky, Ellen J. 2009. "Reflections on Sport, Masculinity, and Nationalism in the Aftermath of 9/11." In *Sexual Sports Rhetoric: Historical and Media Contexts of Violence*, edited by Linda K. Fuller, 63–75. New York: Peter Lang.

St. John, Allen. 2010. *The Billion-Dollar Game: Behind the Scenes of the Greatest Day in American Sport—Super Bowl Sunday*. New York: Anchor.

Summerall, Pat, and Michael Levin. 2010. *Giants: What I Learned about Life from Vince Lombardi and Tom Landry*. Hoboken, NJ: Wiley.

Surowiecki, James. 2019. "Beautiful: Violent. American. The NFL at 100." *New York Times*, December 19, 2019.

Sutel, Seth. 2006. "Cartoons, Violence Inspire Advertisers for Super Bowl XL." *Iowa State Daily*, February 7, 2006.

Sweet, L. 2009. Obama Super Bowl party elected officials invite list. January 30. Available: http://blogs.suntimes.com/sweet/2009/01/obama_super_bowl_party_elected.html.

Taylor, Phil. 2019. "Age of the Megadeal: Do Athletes Make Too Much Money?" *Christian Science Monitor*, May 15, 2019.

Theberge, Nancy. 1981. "A Critique of Critiques: Radical and Feminist Writings on Sport." *Social Forces* 60 (2): 341–353.

TheStarterWife. 2008. "How Not to Throw a Superbowl Party." January 25, 2008. http://ladiesdotdotdot.wordpress.com/2008/01/25/how-not-to-throw-a-superbowl-party.

Thompson, Gabriel. 2016. "I Was a Super Bowl Concession Worker." *Slate*, February 9, 2016.

Tillman, Mary with Narda Zacchino. 2008. *Boots on the Ground by Dusk: My Tribute to Pat Tillman*. California: Tantor Audio.

Trask, Amy, and Mike Freeman. 2016. *You Negotiate Like a Girl: Reflections on a Career in the National Football League*. Chicago: Triumph Books.

Veri, Maria J., and Rita Liberti. 2019. *Gridiron Gourmet: Gender and Food at the Football Tailgate*. Fayetteville, NC: University of Arkansas Press.

Vogan, Travis. 2014. *Keepers of the Flame: NFL Films and the Rise of Sports Media*. Urban: University of Illinois Press.

Von Drehl, David. 2014. "Seeing Is Believing." *Time*, September 22, 2014:20.

Walsh, Bill, Steve Jamison, and Craig Walsh. 2009. *The Score Takes Care of Itself: My Philosophy of Leadership*. New York: Portfolio.

Warren, Matt. 2018. "George H W Bush Told the Nation "Life Goes On" Prior to Super Bowl XXV." *Buffalo Rumblings*, December 4.

Watkins, Steve and Dick Maloney. 2018. *Classic Bengals: The 50 Greatest Games in Cincinnati Bengals History*. Kent, Ohio: The Kent State University Press.

Watson, Tom. 2014. "The Real Super Bowl Question: Should the NFL Be a Nonprofit?" *Forbes*, January 30, 2014.

Weeks, James. 1988. "Football as a Metaphor for War." *American Heritage* 39/6.

Weiss, Don, and Chuck Day. 2003. *The Making of the Super Bowl: The Inside Story of the World's Greatest Sporting Event*. Chicago: Contemporary Books.

Welter, Jen, and Stephanie Krikorian. 2017. *Play Big*. New York: Seal Press.

Wenner, Lawrence A. 1989. "The Super Bowl Pregame Show: Cultural Fantasies and Political Subtext." In *Media, Sport, and Society*, edited by Lawrence A. Wenner, 157–179. Thousand Oaks, CA: Sage.

Wenner, Lawrence A. 2006. "Sports and Media Through the Super Glass Mirror: Placing Blame, Breast-Beating, and a Gaze to the Future." In Raney, Arthur A. and Jennings Bryant (Eds.), *Handbook of Sports and Media*, 47-63. New York: Routledge.

Wenner, Lawrence A. 2008. "Super-Cooled Sports Dirt: Moral Contagion and Super Bowl Commercials in the Shadows of Janet Jackson." *Television & New Media* 9 (2): 131–154.

Wenner, Lawrence A. 2019. "Commodification and Heroic Masculinity: Interrogating Race and the NFL Quarterback in Super Bowl Commercials." In *The Palgrave Handbook of Masculinity and Sport*, edited by Rory Magrath, Jamie Cleland, and Eric Anderson, 225–240. Cham, Switzerland: Palgrave Macmillan, September 5, 2019.

Wenner, Lawrence A., and Stephen J. Jackson, eds. 2009. *Sport, Beer and Gender: Promotional Culture and Contemporary Social Life*. New York: Peter Lang.

Wexell, Jim. 2011. *Pittsburgh Steelers: Men of Steel*. Champaign, IL: Sports Publishing.

Whalen, Dave. 2011. *War and Football: The Gulf War Super Bowl 20 Years Later*. Bleacher Report, January 27, 2011.

Will, George. 2016. "Super Bowl's 60 Minutes of Damage." *The Daily Telegram*.

Willis, Chris. 2010. *The Man Who Built the National Football League: Joe F. Carr*. Lanham, MD: Scarecrow.

Yanity, Molly. 2021. "Apathy and/or Ambivalence?: Women's Sport and Military Promotion." In *Sportswomen's Apparel in the United States: Uniformly Discussed*, edited by Linda K. Fuller, 75–87. Cham, Switzerland: Palgrave Macmillan.

Yao, Deborah. 2009. "Super Bowl Ads Promise Glitz, Groans, Guffaws." *Republican*, January 31, 2009: D4.

Zirin, Dave. 2011. "Sports, Osama, and the New Normal." *Edge of Sports*, May 3, 2011. http://www.edgeofsports.com/2011-05-02-617/index.html.

Zirin, Dave. 2013. *Game Over: How Politics Has Turned the Sports World Upside Down*. New York: The New Press.

Super Bowl-Related Acronyms

ABC	American Broadcasting Company
AFL	American Football League
AFN	American Forces Network
AP	Associated Press
B	Billion
BIPOC	Black, Indigenous or other people of color
BLM	Black Lives Matter
CBS	Columbia Broadcasting System
CRT	Critical race theory
CTE	Chronic traumatic encephalopathy
ESPN	Entertainment and Sports Programming Network
FAIR	Fairness and Accuracy in Reporting
FIFA	International Internationale de Football Association
FSGA	Fantasy Sports & Gaming Association
GBV	Gender-based violence
GCDA	Gendered Critical Discourse Analysis
GOPPPL	Greater Oakland Professional Pigskin Prognosticators League
HBCU	Historically Black College and University
IAAF	International Amateur Athletic Federation
IAMCR	International Association for Mass Communication Research
ILO	International Labor Organization
IEG	Independent Evaluation Group
IOC	International Olympic Committee
LGBTIQ	Lesbian, gay, bisexual, transexual, intersex, queer
M	Million

MEF	Media Education Foundation
MVP	Most Valuable Player
NBC	National Broadcasting Company
NFL	National Football League
NRF	National Retail Federation
NWFA	National Women's Football Association
PASPA	Professional and Amateur Sports Protection Act of 1992
PCA	Popular Culture Association
POC	Person of color

Super Bowl-Related Websites

Arizona Cardinals: azcardinals.com
Atlanta Falcons: atlantafalcons.com
Baltimore Ravens: baltimoreravens.com
Bankrate.com
Buffalo Bills: buffalobills.com
Carolina Panthers: panthers.com
Celebrations.com
Chicago Bears: chicagobears.com
Cincinnati Bengals: bengals.com
Cleveland Browns: clebelandbrowns.com
Dallas Cowboys: dallascowboys.com
Deadspin.com
Denver Broncos: denverbroncos.com
Detroit Lion: detroitlions.com
Entertaining.about.com
ESPN: www.espn.go.com
Fanbuzz.com
Green Bay Packers: packers.com
Houston Texans: houstexans.com
Indianapolis Colts: colts.com
Jacksonville Jaguars: jaguars.com
Kansas City Chiefs: chiefs.com
Las Vegas Raiders: raiders.com
Legalsuperbowlbetting.com
Los Angeles Chargers: chargers.com
Los Angeles Rams: therams.com
Miami Dolphins: miamidolphins.com

Minnesota Vikings: Vikings.com
National Football League: www.nfl.com
New England Patriots: patriots.com
New Orleans Saints: neworleanssaints.com
New York Giants: giants.com
New York Jets: newyorkjets.com
NFLgirluk.com
Philadelphia Eagles: philadelphiaeagles.com
Pittsburgh Steelers: steelers.com
Pro Football Hall of Fame: www.profootballhof.com
Pro Football Reference: www.pro-football-reference.com
San Francisco 49ers: 49ers.com
Seattle Seahawks: seahawks.com
Sportsbettingdime.com
TheSportsGeek.com
Sports Illustrated: www.si.com
Super Bowl history: www.superbowlhistory.net
Tampa Bay Buccaneers: buccaneers.com
Tennessee Titans: tennesseetitans.com
Vince Lombardi official website: www.vincelombardi.com
Washington Redskins: redskins.com

Super Bowl Championships

#	Date	Teams & Scores	Venue	Attendance
I	1/15/67	Green Bay Packers v Kansas City Chiefs 35-10	Los Angeles, CA	61,946
II	1/14/68	Green Bay Packers v Oakland Raiders 33-14	Miami, FL	75,546
III	1/12/69	New York Jets v Baltimore Colts 16-7	Miami, FL	75,389
IV	1/11/70	Kansas City Chiefs v Minnesota Vikings 23-7	New Orleans, LA	80,562
V	1/17/71	Baltimore Colts v Dallas Cowboys 16-13	Miami, FL	79,204
VI	1/16/72	Dallas Cowboys v Miami Dolphins 24-3	New Orleans, LA	81,023
VII	1/14/73	Miami Dolphins v Washington Redskins 14-7	Los Angeles, CA	90,182

#	Date	Teams & Scores	Venue	Attendance
VIII	1/13/74	Miami Dolphins v Minnesota Vikings 24-7	Houston, TX	71,882
IX	1/12/75	Pittsburgh Steelers v Minnesota Vikings 16-6	New Orleans, LA	80,997
X	1/18/76	Pittsburgh Steelers v Dallas Cowboys 21-17	Miami, FL	80,187
XI	1/9/77	Oakland Raiders v Minnesota Vikings 32-14	Pasadena, CA	103,438
XII	1/15/78	Dallas Cowboys v Denver Broncos 27-10	New Orleans, LA	76,400
XIII	1/21/79	Pittsburgh Steelers v Dallas Cowboys 35-31	Miami, FL	79,484
XIV	1/20/80	Pittsburgh Steelers v Los Angeles Rams 31-19	Pasadena, CA	103,985
XV	1/25/81	Oakland Raiders v Philadelphia Eagles 27-10	New Orleans, LA	73,135
XVI	1/24/82	San Francisco 49ers v Cincinnati Bengals 26-21	Pontiac, MI	81,270
XVII	1/30/83	Washington Redskins v Miami Dolphins 27-17	Pasadena, CA	103,667

#	Date	Teams & Scores	Venue	Attendance
XVIII	1/22/84	Los Angeles Raiders v Washington Redskins 38-9	Tampa, FL	72,920
XIX	1/20/85	San Francisco 49ers v Miami Dolphins 38-16	Stanford, CA	84,059
XX	1/26/86	Chicago Bears v New England Patriots 46-10	New Orleans, LA	73,818
XXI	1/25/87	New York Giants v Denver Broncos 39-20	Pasadena, CA	101,063
XXII	1/31/88	Washington Redskins v Denver Broncos 42-10	San Diego, CA	73,302
XXIII	1//22/89	San Francisco 49ers v Cincinnati Bengals 20-16	Miami, FL	75,129
XXIV	1/28/90	San Francisco 49ers vs Denver Broncos 55-10	New Orleans, LA	72,919
XXV	1/27/91	New York Giants v Buffalo Bills 20-19	Tampa, FL	73,813
XXVI	1/26/92	Washington Redskins v Buffalo Bills 37-14	Minneapolis, MN	63,130
XXVII	1/31/93	Dallas Cowboys v Buffalo Bills 52-17	Pasadena, CA	98,374

#	Date	Teams & Scores	Venue	Attendance
XXVIII	1/30/94	Dallas Cowboys v Buffalo Bills 30-13	Atlanta, GA	72,817
XXIX	1/29/95	San Francisco 49ers v San Diego Chargers 49-26	Miami, FL	74,107
XXX	1/28/96	Dallas Cowboys v Pittsburgh Steelers 27-17	Tempe, AZ	76,347
XXXI	1/26/97	Green Bay Packers v New England Patriots 35-21	New Orleans, LA	72,301
XXXII	1/25/98	Denver Broncos v Green Bay Packers 31-24	San Diego, CA	68,912
XXXIII	1/31/99	Denver Broncos v Atlanta Falcons 34-19	Miami, FL	74,803
XXXIV	1/30/2000	St. Louis Rams v Tennessee Titans 23-16	Atlanta, GA	72,625
XXXV	1/28/01	Baltimore Ravens v New York Giants 34-7	Tampa, FL	71,921
XXXVI	2/3/02	New England Patriots v St. Louis Rams 20-17	New Orleans, LA	72,922
XXXVII	1/26/03	Tampa Bay Buccaneers v Oakland Raiders 48-21	San Diego, CA	67,603

#	Date	Teams & Scores	Venue	Attendance
XXXVIII	2/1/04	New England Patriots v Carolina Panthers 32-29	Houston, TX	71,525
XXXIX	2/6/05	New England Patriots v Philadelphia Eagles 24-21	Jacksonville, FL	78,125
XL	2/5/06	Pittsburgh Steelers v Seattle Seahawks 21-10	Detroit, MI	68,206
XLI	2/4/07	Indianapolis Colts v Chicago Bears 29-17	Miami, FL	74,512
XLII	2/3/08	New York Giants v New England Patriots 17-14	Glendale, AZ	71,101
XLIII	2/1/09	Pittsburgh Steelers v Arizona Cardinals 27-23	Tampa, FL	70,774
XLIV	2/7/10	New Orleans Saints v Indianapolis Colts 31-17	Miami, FL	74,059
XLV	2/6/11	Green Bay Packers v Pittsburgh Steelers 31-25	Arlington, TX	103,219
XLVI	2/5/12	New York Giants v New England Patriots 21-17	Indianapolis, IN	68,658

#	Date	Teams & Scores	Venue	Attendance
XLVII	2/3/13	Baltimore Ravens v San Francisco 49ers 34-31	New Orleans, LA	71,024
XLVIII	2/2/14	Seattle Seahawks v Denver Broncos 43-8	East Rutherford, NJ	82,529
XLXI	2/1/15	New England Patriots v Seattle Seahawks 28-24	Glendale, AZ	70,288
L	2/7/16	Denver Broncos v Carolina Panthers 24-10	Santa Clara, CA	71,088
LI	2/5/17	New England Patriots v Atlanta Falcons 34-28	Houston, TX	70,807
LII	2/4/18	Philadelphia Eagles v New England Patriots 41-33	Minneapolis, MN	67,612
LIII	2/3/19	New England Patriots v Los Angeles Rams 13-3	Atlanta, GA	70,081
LIV	2/2/20	Kansas City Chiefs v San Francisco 49ers 31-20	Miami, FL	62,417
LV	2/7/21	Tampa Bay Buccaneers v Kansas City Chiefs 31-9	Tampa, FL	24,835
LVI	2/13/22	Los Angeles Rams v Cincinnati Bengals 23-20	Inglewood, CA	70,048

Super Bowl MVPs

Year	#	Winner	Team	Position
1967	I	Bart Starr	Green Bay Packers	Quarterback
1968	II	Bart Starr	Green Bay Packers	Quarterback
1969	III	Joe Namath	New York Jets	Quarterback
1970	IV	Len Dawson	Kansas City Chiefs	Quarterback
1971	V	Chuck Howley	Dallas Cowboys	Linebacker
1972	VI	Roger Staubach	Dallas Cowboys	Quarterback
1973	VII	Jack Scott	Miami Dolphins	Safety
1974	VIII	Larry Csonka	Miami Dolphins	Running back
1975	IX	Franco Harris	Pittsburgh Steelers	Running back
1976	X	Lynn Swann	Pittsburgh Steelers	Wide receiver
1977	XI	Fred Bilent-nikoff	Oakland Raiders	Wide receiver
1978	XII	Harvey Martin	Dallas Cowboys	Defensive end
1978	XII	Randy White	Dallas Cowboys	Defensive tackle
1979	XIII	Terry Bradshaw	Pittsburgh Steelers	Quarterback
1980	XIV	Terry Bradshaw	Pittsburgh Steelers	Quarterback
1981	XV	Jim Plunkett	Oakland Raiders	Quarterback
1982	XVI	Joe Montana	San Francisco 49ers	Quarterback
1983	XVII	John Riggins	Washington Redskins	Running back
1984	XVIII	Marcus Allen	Los Angeles Raiders	Running back
1985	XIX	Joe Montana	San Francisco 49ers	Quarterback
1986	XX	Richard Dent	Chicago Bears	Defensive end
1987	XXI	Phil Simms	New York Giants	Quarterback

Year	#	Winner	Team	Position
1988	XXII	Doug Williams	Washington Redskins	Quarterback
1989	XXIII	Jerry Rice	San Francisco 49ers	Wide receiver
1990	XXIV	Joe Montana	San Francisco 49ers	Quarterback
1991	XXV	Ottis Anderson	New York Giants	Running back
1992	XXVI	Mark Rypian	Washington Redskins	Quarterback
1993	XXVII	Troy Aikman	Dallas Cowboys	Quarterback
1994	XXVIII	Emmitt Smith	Dallas Cowboys	Quarterback
1995	XXIX	Steve Young	San Francisco 49ers	Quarterback
1996	XXX	Larry Brown	Dallas Cowboys	Cornerback
1997	XXXI	Desmond Howard	Green Bay Packers	Kick returner
1998	XXXII	Terrell Davis	Denver Broncos	Running back
1999	XXXIII	John Elway	Denver Broncos	Quarterback
2000	XXXIV	Kurt Warner	St. Louis Rams	Quarterback
2001	XXXV	Ray Lewis	Baltimore Ravens	Linebacker
2002	XXXVI	Tom Brady	New England Patriots	Quarterback
2003	XXXVII	Dexter Jackson	Tampa Bay Buccaneers	Safety
2004	XXXVIII	Tom Brady	New England Patriots	Quarterback
2005	XXXIX	Deion Branch	New England Patriots	Wide receiver
2006	XL	Hines Ward	Pittsburgh Steelers	Wide receiver
2007	XLI	Peyton Manning	Indianapolis Colts	Quarterback
2008	XLII	Eli Manning	New York Giants	Quarterback
2009	XLIII	Santonio Holmes	Pittsburgh Steelers	Wide receiver
2010	XLIV	Drew Brees	New Orleans Saints	Quarterback
2011	XLV	Aaron Rodgers	Green Bay Packers	Quarterback
2012	XLVI	Eli Manning	New York Giants	Quarterback
2013	XLVII	Joe Flacco	Baltimore Ravens	Quarterback
2014	XLVIII	Malcolm Smith	Seattle Seahawks	Linebacker

Year	#	Winner	Team	Position
2015	XLXI	Tom Brady	New England Patriots	Quarterback
2016	L	Von Miller	Denver Broncos	Linebacker
2017	LI	Tom Brady	New England Patriots	Quarterback
2018	LII	Nick Foles	Philadelphia Eagles	Quarterback
2019	LIII	Julian Edelman	New England Patriots	Wide receiver
2020	LIV	Patrick Mahomes	Kansas City Chiefs	Quarterback
2021	LV	Tom Brady	Tampa Bay Buccaneers	Quarterback
2022	LVI	Cooper Kupp	Los Angeles Rams	Wide receiver

Super Bowl Team Wins

Team	Winning Years	# of Wins
Arizona Cardinals		-
Atlanta Falcons		-
Baltimore Colts	1971	1
Baltimore Ravens	2001, 2013	2
Buffalo Bills		-
Carolina Panthers		-
Chicago Bears	1986	1
Cincinnati Bengals		-
Cleveland Browns		-
Dallas Cowboys	1972, 1978, 1993, 1994, 1996	5
Denver Broncos	1998, 1999, 2016	3
Green Bay Packers	1967, 1968, 1997, 2011	4
Indianapolis Colts	2007	1
Kansas City Chiefs	1970, 2020	2
Los Angeles Raiders	1984	1
Los Angeles Rams	2022	1
Miami Dolphins	1973, 1974	2
Minnesota Vikings		-
New England Patriots	2002, 2004, 2005, 2015, 2017, 2019	6
New Orleans Saints	2010	1
New York Giants	1987, 1991, 2008, 2012	4
New York Jets	1969	1
Oakland Raiders	1977, 1981	2
Philadelphia Eagles	2018	1
Pittsburgh Steelers	1975, 1976, 1979, 1980, 2006, 2009	6

Team	Winning Years	# of Wins
San Diego Chargers		-
San Francisco 49ers	1982, 1985, 1989, 1990, 1995	5
Seattle Seahawks	2014	1
St. Louis Rams	2000	1
Tampa Bay Buccaneers	2003, 2021	2
Washington Redskins	1983, 1988, 1992	3

Super Bowl Host Cities

Host City	Year(s) hosting	#
Arlington, TX	2011	1
Atlanta, GA	1994, 2000, 2019	3
Detroit, MI	2006	1
East Rutherford, NJ	2014	1
Glendale, AZ	2008, 2015	2
Houston, TX	1974, 2004, 2017	3
Indianapolis, IN	2012	1
Jacksonville, FL	2005	1
Los Angeles, CA	1967, 1973, 2022	3
Miami, FL	1968, 1969, 1971, 1976, 1979, 1989, 1995, 1999, 2007, 2010, 2020	11
Minneapolis, MN	1992, 2018	2
New Orleans, LA	1970, 1972, 1975, 1978, 1981, 1986, 1990, 1997, 2002, 2013	10
Pasadena, CA	1977, 1980, 1983, 1987, 1993	5
Pontiac, MI	1982	1
Santa Clara, CA	2016	1
Stanford, CA	1985	1
San Diego, CA	1988, 1998, 2003	3
Tampa, FL	1984, 1991, 2001, 2009, 2021	5
Tempe, AZ	1996	1

Super Bowl Costs for 30-second Commercials

Year	Cost of a 30-second commercial
1967	$37,500/$42,500 (multiple networks)
1968	$54,500
1969	$55,000
1970	$78,200
1971	$72,500
1972	$86,100
1973	$88,100
1974	$103,500
1975	$107,000
1976	$110,000
1977	$125,000
1978	$162,300
1979	$185,000
1980	$222,000
1981	$275,000
1982	$324,300
1983	$400,000
1984	$368,200
1985	$525,000
1986	$550,000
1987	$600,000
1988	$645,500
1989	$675,500
1990	$700,400

1991	$800,000
1992	$850,000
1993	$850,000
1994	$900,000
1995	$1,150,000
1996	$1,085,000
1997	$1,200,000
1998	$1,291,100
1999	$1,600,000
2000	$2,100,000
2001	$2,200,000
2002	$2,200,000
2003	$2,200,000
2004	$2,302,200
2005	$2,400,000
2006	$2,500,000
2007	$2,385,365
2008	$2,699,963
2009	$2,000,960
2010	$2,945,010
2011	$3,100,000
2012	$3,500,000
2013	$3,800,000
2014	$4,000,000
2015	$4,250,000
2016	$4,500,000
2017	$5,000,000
2018	$5,200,000
2019	$5,300,000
2020	$5,560,000
2021	$5,500,000
2022	$6,600.000
2023	$7,000,000

(Source: Nielsen Media Research: Superbowl-ads.com)

INDEX

ABOUT THE AUTHOR

Linda K. Fuller (PhD, University of Massachusetts), Professor Emerita of Communications at Worcester State University, is the author/(co-)editor of more than thirty books—including *Sport, Rhetoric, and Gender* (2006), *Sportscasters/Sportscasting* (2008), the two-volume *Sexual Sports Rhetoric* (2009), *The Power of Global Community Media* (2012), *Female Olympians* (2016), *Female Olympian and Paralympian Events* (2018), the two-volume *Sportswomen's Apparel* (USA and global, 2021), and *Female Olympian and Paralympian athlete activists* (20023). The recipient of Fulbright awards to teach in Singapore and to do HIV/AIDS research in Senegal, check out her website: https://www.LK-Fullersport.com.

Garry Whannel, Emeritus Professor of Media Cultures, University of Bedfordshire, UK, *Understanding the Olympics* (Routledge 2020)

Celebrating the Super Bowl, by Linda K. Fuller, offers a fascinating account of the cultural rituals of Super Bowl parties. The communal and celebratory is placed within the context of the history, politics, and economics of this mega-event. In particular, Fuller examines the masculinist ethos of the future of American football and its dark underbelly of sexual violence. Ritual celebration is the heart of this absorbing account. Ranging across parking lot tailgate parties, home barbecues, and celebrity-studded spectaculars, Fuller charts the massive consumption of food and drink, the settings in which it takes place, and the conventions that shape the rituals. As a keen cook, she even manages to include several recipes.

Elizabeth Gregg, JAIDE Institute, University of North Florida

Linda K. Fuller's *Celebrating the Super Bowl* is a wonderful addition to existing texts dedicated to what has become the largest and one of the most profitable days of the year in America. Unlike many others dedicated to the topic, Dr. Fuller's version is more than just a coffee table book; it chronicles the history of the game, broadcasting, the introduction of social media and related impact, and the importance of Super Bowl parties for the nation and for casual fans alike. While Dr. Fuller does include records of the Super Bowl and other player statistics, the real strength of the book lies in the factual knowledge of how the greatest spectacle on Earth has evolved contained within. From football fans to students studying sport, all will find a tremendous resource and endless entertainment in Dr. Fuller's latest text. For the football fan, this book is a must have.

Danielle Sarver Coombs, Kent State University and Anne C. Osborne, Syracuse University, Co-Editors of the *Routledge Handbook of Sport Fans and Fandom*

"No single event in the United States draws attention quite like the Super Bowl. Both the game itself and the cultural traditions around it are embedded in the American psyche, and Fuller's book does a wonderful job exploring the history and influence of the 'The Big Game.' This book is an excellent resource for those interested in better understanding how the Super Bowl is celebrated—and why we should care."

Katerina Tovia-Dufoo, Sport Sociology, Victoria University of Wellington, New Zealand

Expecting another typical book about Super Bowl? Dead wrong. This book is written in a brilliant way that pulls in the reader from the start with its homely recipe where it's able to take you back to those good ol' sporting moments. From the buffalo wings to the guac, it takes one on a serious and fun journey of wanting to understand just that extra bit more about the Super Bowl and ALL the "hoopla" and mega-event shenanigans. This book oozed a real sense of loyalty, passion, and belonging to a phenomenon even if one is not from the United States. From a traditional sports-crazy nation to another, this book showed up ready to party.

www.ingramcontent.com/pod-product-compliance
Lightning Source LLC
Chambersburg PA
CBHW040423110426
42814CB00008B/334